The
Southern Way

The regular volume for the Southern devotee

Kevin Robertson

Issue 36

www.crecy.co.uk

© 2016 Crécy Publishing Ltd
and the various contributors

ISBN 9781909328594

First published in 2016 by Noodle Books
an imprint of Crécy Publishing Ltd

All editorial submissions to:
The Southern Way (Kevin Robertson)
Conway
Warnford Rd
Corhampton
Hants SO32 3ND
Tel: 01489 877880
editorial@thesouthernway.co.uk

A CIP record for this book is available from the
British Library

Publisher's note: Every effort has been made to
identify and correctly attribute photographic
credits. Any error that may have occurred is
entirely unintentional.
In line with the new design the front cover image has
changed from that originally advertised. All other
information is unaffected.

Printed in Malta by Gutenberg Press Ltd

Noodle Books is an imprint of
Crécy Publishing Limited
1a Ringway Trading Estate
Shadowmoss Road
Manchester M22 5LH

www.crecy.co.uk

Issue No 37 of THE SOUTHERN WAY
ISBN 978-1-909328-61-7
available in January 2017 at £14.95
To receive your copy the moment it is
released, order in advance from your usual
supplier, or it can be sent post-free (UK)
direct from the publisher:

Crécy Publishing Ltd

1a Ringway Trading Estate, Shadowmoss
Road, Manchester M22 5LH

Tel 0161 499 0024

www.crecy.co.uk

enquiries@crecy.co.uk

Front Cover:
**Bulleid power at Waterloo: one can almost smell the
hot oil that would have been around. In the background
is No 34064** *Fighter Command*, **while nearest the
camera stands No 34018** *Axminster. Lawrence Hassall,
Kevin Robertson collection*

Rear Cover:
**The three-cylinder Maunsell 'Mogul', in the form of
(right) 'U1' No 31901 and (left) two-cylinder 'N' No
31831, at Ashford. Something in the right background
may also be of note – part of a cab sheet numbered '…
4012'. So where was No 34012 Launceston at this time?
Presumably under repair. Certainly those are Bulleid
wheels in the foreground.**

Title page:
**For whatever reason, some engines appear to have
attracted the camera and others not so. One that certainly
falls into the latter category is No 34049** *Anti-Aircraft
Command*, **a regretted early casualty of the 'Battle of
Britain' Class that was withdrawn in December 1963 (there
are conflicting dates exactly when in December this took
place, so it's probably best to restrict it to the month
alone). A Salisbury-based engine from 1951 until its
demise, this machine, together with No 34035, was the
subject of experiments with varying types of
casing/cowling modifications in an attempt to reduce
drifting smoke and steam obstructing the driver's view
ahead. The red background to the nameplate will be noted.**

Contents

The unmistakable outline of 'USA' No 30064 outside the front of Eastleigh shed. A recently discovered data sheet reposing at the NRM dated 23 March 1963*, reveals that BR had plans to replace a number of 'home-grown' SR types with imports from other areas, the idea being seemingly to limit the number of small classes as well as provide employment for engines now redundant from elsewhere, although not considered life-expired. As is known, a number of LMS Class 2MT tanks did in fact arrive as replacements for the 'M7s', the two remaining 'E2s' and three remaining 'E4s', but some of the other intended exchanges did not take place: five surviving members of the 'AIX' Class were to be replaced by LMS 'Dock tanks', the 'W' Class by the redundant GWR '56xx' 0-6-2T type, the 'S15' Class superseded either by 'WD' 2-8-0 or LMS 4F 0-6-0 engines (the 4Fs would also serve as a replacement for all 'Q' and Q1' engines), and the 'USA' Class replaced by LNER 'J50' tank engines. It was noted that at this time no inroads were envisaged into the ranks of the Bulleid 'Pacifics', and there were to be no transfers of larger steam engines to the SR from other regions. (One can also almost imagine the reaction of some seriously unhappy enginemen and fitters being lumbered with 'WDs' and 4Fs. Picture in your mind also the thought of an LMS 'Dock tank' taking three loaded coaches from Hayling to Havant!) *Bob Treacher*

* The items consists of three sheets each with columns marked: 'Class', 'Type', 'Book stock at 23-3-1963', 'Proposed withdrawals', 'Stock remaining' and 'Proposed reallocation to secure elimination of type'. There is one attached heading sheet marked 'Reallocations Part 2'; can we assume that 'Part 1' (which was not located) was issued in 1962 and had led to the withdrawal/elimination of several complete classes?

Introduction

It is always good to be able to report something new. After almost 50 years since steam ended on the Southern Region, 68 years since nationalisation and 91 years since the SECR, LBSCR and LSWR were formed into the Southern Railway, it might be thought what is there left to say, but I can categorically answer 'quite a lot'. The reader will gather I am in a numbers mood as I write this.

Regular readers (sufferers) of my missives will be aware how I am continually harking on about searching for odd snippets of information, whether historical facts or reminiscences, and on both counts we have certainly come up trumps recently. Accordingly you will note several news topics this month, two of which I feel stand out: the reminiscences supplied by Dennis Upton and the lost images of Stephen Townroe, the latter the first of several. I will admit that a few months ago I was slightly concerned how to follow Charles Anderson, which concluded in July – thank you all for your plaudits here – but I do feel we have a pair of worthy successors, which it has been both a pleasure and privilege to include.

In addition, some files on locomotive matters 'came my way' earlier in the year, and one that is included this time is an unfortunate event involving a 'C' Class engine – see page 21. While it certainly provides information on a previously forgotten incident, it is also interesting to note that the report contained no reference to the crew involved, although information on this topic was found in a different source. Compared with today's 'risk-assessed' and 'health and safety'-conscious life, railwaymen took the hazards associated with their work merely as something to be accepted, although it is a salutary warning that steam under pressure is not something to be trifled with.

Which leads me to my next question, and one I ask myself time and time again: how much 'old' history do I dare include within these pages? To put my own views forward let me say immediately that I am a subscriber to three email discussion groups on the internet. The SEMG (Southern Email Group) is excellent – I do not contribute to discussion for the simple reason that I cannot for the life of me remember my username or password (mental note: *must* do something about both one day), but it is still a useful tool to see what is 'hot' in both the discussion and interest topics. I suppose also being of pensionable age, I should accept that there are bound to be those whose own knowledge is not as great as others, but there are also others whose areas of expertise are both wide and extraordinary. So do we at 'SW' and elsewhere attempt to provide just unpublished topics or should we also be affording material to those who wish to build up their own knowledge database? Hence the dichotomy facing an editor. I suspect I am not alone in having the proverbial sleepless nights on the same topic.

Let me close this piece with a true story. Travelling by SWT recently in the evening rush hour (and standing for most of the way), I and my fellow passengers became aware of an elderly gentleman standing near one of the doorways and he was clearly in some distress. A fellow passenger who was closer attempted to assist only to discover that this was the first time the said gentlemen had travelled by train for what was several decades, after just about managing to find his train and pass through the barrier with (so it appeared) some assistance. He had in fact been carried far beyond his destination because he had been unable to work out how to open the doors. He was now having another go, this time in the reverse direction. I should add that he gave no impression of being at all senile and was also bemoaning that the last time he had travelled there were compartments, and toilets were also available. Change can be subtle sometimes, and unless we keep a regular look-out that same change can also overtake us.

Kevin Robertson

Dennis Upton
From Fireman to Lineman

Mike Upton

It is always gratifying to recall a railwayman's reminiscences that are in some way different, and the story of Dennis Upton certainly fits into that category. Starting work on the Southern Region in March 1954 – he already had some railway experience on the GWR prior to 1948 – Dennis progressed with the locomotive department at Basingstoke from the ground upwards, and this is the first time we have been able to record any reminiscences of a man from this depot. Circumstances dictated that his footplate time would be cut short, but not his railway life, as he subsequently found a new path with the Signalling & Telegraph Department, a route that would continue until retirement. Such a crossover was certainly unusual, but thanks to his son Mike Upton and also to Pat Butler, who

suggested the idea in the first place, we can enjoy some of the tales and experiences he endured.

Basingstoke 'C' signal box – the former GWR cabin that stood in the 'V' between the SR and GWR lines at the station – is recorded in its final months (or perhaps even weeks/days); the replacement MAS panel box is the white building on the right. The Southern influence – the former GWR line as far as Southcote Junction south of Reading – is apparent, with green and yellow paintwork on the steps and windows. The SR had taken control of the Reading line in 1950. Following MAS, the top of the box was literally knocked off and the base converted into a workshop for the S&T technicians and officially used for maintenance of components for the air-points. Apart from railway-related items, repairs to bicycles and other non-railway objects were similarly dealt with! *Tony Woodforth collection*

Dennis Geoffrey Upton was born at home in Pamber Heath (North Hampshire) on 29 September 1930, the younger of the two boys of Lillian and Bill Upton. His was not a railway family, his father being a builder.

As his character developed through childhood, so did an interest in railways, as was also the case but perhaps to a slightly lesser extent with his older brother Ted. Later the two of them would spend hours by the lineside at places such as Aldermaston. Later still, and while at school, Dennis was able to earn some money working for the local grocer and also the butcher's shop.

Leaving Tadley Council School at the age of 14, Dennis had a single ambition, to work on the railway, and in particular to be an engine driver. At this time (1944) and notwithstanding a general shortage of staff even towards the end of the war, railway positions were still obtained largely through family connections and of course Dennis had none.

Assistance, however, would come from an unlikely quarter. At the time, Dennis's father was in the local Home Guard, which involved guarding the railway yards at Basingstoke. For his day job as a builder he was engaged at the temporary headquarters of the GWR at Aldermaston, where, on behalf of his son, he made contact with a senior GWR man. The result was that Dennis was offered a position as cleaner at Reading (GWR) shed. We know little about what was destined to be a short spell here, for unfortunately his mother was seriously ill and, with his father away from home much of the time and brother Ted serving in the forces, Dennis felt it better to try and get a transfer nearer to home. The result was a transfer to the Traffic Department and the post of lad-porter at Bramley, destined to be the start of a long relationship with the Basingstoke to Reading (later Southern Region) line.

Dennis recalls that, at the time, Bramley had a staff of nineteen with the station open from early morning until after midnight. Adjacent was the military's central ammunition depot, which was very busy throughout the 24-hour period. Indeed, so intense was security in the area that more than once he was asked for his identification when cycling to and from work.

Dennis remained at Bramley until 1949, including the change from being a GWR man to an employee of the Western Region. Then came call-up for national service and for this he was directed to report to Bulford, alighting from the train at Salisbury and being herded towards a 3-ton truck under the instruction of (as Dennis puts it) '...a horrible little NCO whose language cannot be repeated.' Notwithstanding this first brush with junior military authority, army life would suit Dennis, for he signed on after his compulsory two years, ending up as a corporal in the RMP regiment assigned to Montgomery's security staff in France. Upon leaving, he was given a photograph of the great man, signed in the special green ink Montgomery kept for personal correspondence.

With a return to Civvy Street, Dennis contacted Mr Wix, shedmaster at Basingstoke, and was successful in obtaining a position there as cleaner earning £5 10s 6d for a 48-hour week and a promised rise to £5 19s when appointed fireman. This was in March 1954.

Basingstoke in the early 1950s. The shed stood at the west end of the station on a site north of the main line. It was certainly not unique when it came to both servicing and preparing engines in less than ideal conditions, as witness here with '700' No 30368 being worked on outside under the wheel hoist. This was the engine on which Dennis was regularly firing at the time his son Michael was born. *Paul Hersey collection*

Already aged 24, Dennis had starting cleaning at a somewhat older age than most, and as a result his 'apprenticeship' (learning about engines) was somewhat different. Instead of shifts as a cleaner, he spent two weeks with the fitting staff, two weeks with the steam-raisers and a final week riding on engines. He was then interviewed by Inspector Baden Pope and passed straight for firing, commensurate also with that welcome pay rise.

Conditions for the footplatemen at Basingstoke were, to say the least, primitive, but then this was the case for most sheds everywhere. Lighting inside the shed (which was a dead-end building) was very poor. Outside at night was equally bad, with obstacles of all kinds intended to catch out the unwary. Messing was similarly basic: a cabin with wooden seats, a table, an open fire and a cold water tap. Not unexpectedly there was a constantly boiling kettle, the simple rule being that if you used water from the kettle you were the one who refilled it.

At the time Basingstoke had an allocation of thirty locomotives with eighty sets of footplatemen. In addition were the fitters, steam-raisers, storemen, and office staff. There was also a snowplough!

Dennis recalls that his first firing job was in the very busy goods yards at Basingstoke. There were three yards: 'down west' for traffic for Southampton and the West of England, 'up west' for traffic to Nine Elms and Feltham, and 'north' for traffic to the Midlands and the North via the GWR. Two engines were regularly used on these shunt duties; one was 'G6' No 30258 and the other was any one of the 'M7s'

allocated to the depot. Such was the volume of traffic that Dennis recalls he was lucky to get a break, and it was the norm to eat while you worked. It was the same if rostered for shed duties, making sure engines were coaled, watered, turned and placed ready for the next duty. 'We were always being chased by the shed foreman, who somehow always knew where to find us.' Dennis recalls one occasion (but not the date or actual locomotive) when a shedman shunting an engine out of steam ready for the fitters left it, forgetting to put on the handbrake – it rolled straight through the end wall of the shed, fortunately without injury.

One day, when rostered as 'spare', a fireman in the top link went sick. The duty to be covered was that of a 'Remembrance' Class 'N15X' 4-6-0, No 32332 *Stroudley*, working a passenger service from Basingstoke to Waterloo. Dennis had never been on the main line before and was very glad of the tips given to him by the driver. He recalls an extremely rough-riding engine with a need to hang on when passing over points and crossings.

'There was dust everywhere, an indescribable noise accompanied by vibration and alternate hot and cold. I had to use hand signals to attract the driver's attention as it was difficult to make oneself heard.'

Later his experience was to broaden even more, for after their engine had been released at Waterloo they made their way to Nine Elms for a break and it was here that he was introduced to the art of breakfast cooked on the firing shovel … there would be many more in later years!

'G6' No 30258 shunts at Basingstoke. This was the first engine on which Dennis fired. He also worked over the short remaining section of the Basingstoke & Alton light railway, a portion of which had been retained to serve the Thorneycroft works. The last section of this line, albeit disused for many years, can still be seen in 2016 curving away at the west end of what was the former down yard. *John Davenport*

Dennis was of the opinion that Basingstoke seemed to get everyone's unwanted engines. Later, and with experience, Dennis would come to regard the 'Remembrance' Class as his favourite type. He would also visit Nine Elms many times in the future for his loco to be coaled and watered, although every time when under the coaling stage it was with anticipation that they waited to see what would fall into the tender. Too often it was mainly a huge cloud of dust, which meant a tender full of briquettes and dust and a rough run home shovelling the remnants of the coal, this having broken up after being dropped from the height of the Nine Elms coaling tower. There was no South Wales steam coal in this part of London.

'Remembrance' Class 4-6-0 No 32331 *Beattie*, sister engine to No 32332 on which Dennis had his first main-line turn, and also his personal favourite type. He recalls that they were rough-riders and on their last legs by the time he experienced them – he also states that most of Basingstoke's allocation were in poor condition. All seven members of the 'Remembrance' Class were allocated there throughout their BR existence; No 32331 was destined to be the last in service, being withdrawn in July 1957. *Photographer unknown*

Another time on an up train from Basing (Basingstoke was always shortened to 'Basing' by railwaymen), Dennis and his driver had a particularly good run to Waterloo and, while tidying the footplate, a city gent came up to the driver and said something along the lines of 'Well done, old chap, jolly good run…', and gave the driver a 10 shilling note – a lot of money in the mid-fifties. The driver shared it with Dennis; he was an example of the comradeship of the footplate, although Dennis commented that some drivers would have kept it all themselves. As for the fate of any fireman who allowed the safety valves of his engine to lift under the hallowed roof of Waterloo, it was certain he would be spoken to either by the motive power foreman based there or at his depot before booking off.

Freight turns were frequent duties. One turn left Basingstoke for Eastleigh, usually with an 'S15'. This was around lunchtime, the schedule being sufficient to reach Allbrook (north of Eastleigh) ahead of the down 'Bournemouth Belle'. Having collected the loco from the shed, they would take it to the down yard and couple up to a long freight on a siding behind the 'West' signal box (renamed 'B' in 1950 but still referred to as 'West' box). There was a set of trailing crossovers that connected the shed with the 'down west' yard. These were used to access the shed as well as allowing engines to take up whatever duty they were allocated. Near the shed end of the crossover was a wooden box mounted on a post that contained a bell-push used to communicate with 'B' box and so advise the signalman where the engine was destined for. At busy times, such as on summer Saturdays, a man was stationed here to operate the bell and so avoid the need for the fireman to get off the engine. The codes were such that, on receipt, the signalman could set the corresponding road for the engine. Dennis believes that there may also have been communication from here with 'C' box (the old Great Western box) for locos going along the up reception and 'round the back' to the former GWR Platform 6.

Before setting the road towards Worting on this freight turn, the signalman would generally ask the driver if all was OK; if the driver replied that the engine was good, the signalman would let the train go; any other response and the train would he held until the 'Belle' had passed. Dennis recalls that his driver was perhaps a shade optimistic on occasions and recalls seeing the signalman at Weston, less than halfway to Eastleigh from Basingstoke, leaning out and frantically gesturing to them to hurry up. There was of course always the option of slowing the train and diverting it into the loop at Wallers Ash, but to do so was a gamble – whether it would in fact delay the 'Belle' longer than by letting the freight continue, especially as it was downhill all the way to Eastleigh. The same gesturing would occur at some of the other signal boxes, notably Winchester Junction, Winchester City, St Cross and finally Shawford Junction, no one wanting to be responsible for delaying the following train. They would eventually 'get inside' at Allbrook, the 'Belle' passing through shortly after, accompanied by a blow on the whistle to show that the driver of the 'Merchant Navy' was not amused at having the various distant signals pulled late. Traffic regulation old style! As an aside, this shows how well the signallers must have known individual drivers, or at least their ability to keep time – real trust, as delaying the 'Belle' would indeed mean a 'please explain'.

They also worked banana trains north from Southampton Docks. Upon notification from Control that a ship had docked, the foreman at Basingstoke would dispatch a crew to the Docks, often with a 'U' Class, where, after turning, they would wait in the enginemen's cabin until the foreman came in to ask, 'Anyone know the road to…?' Fortunately Basingstoke men, especially those from the former GWR shed who by now had been amalgamated into the SR, had accumulated a wide route knowledge, not only to London but also to Reading and the Midlands. Dennis worked with one such former GWR man at the time and they could be off to places such as Bordesley, West London GW, or even on to the Great Central via the connection at Banbury. This could then result in a long day, after which they normally came back to Basingstoke light – unless of course Control found something for them to work back. Mike Upton also adds, 'The ex-Western men generally resented having to be amalgamated (taken over) by the old enemy (the Southern). It has always intrigued me that despite footplatemen being almost to a man staunch union and Labour men, so many of them had very strong loyalties to their respective old companies.'

The return working might be an overnight freight off the Great Central, which they would probably pick up at Banbury. If this was a train conveying fish vans from Grimsby, some could be dropped off at Moreton Cutting and Reading West Junction, thence on to Basingstoke where a single van was detached and the crew relieved. Fish caught one day was in the shops the next morning, the Basingstoke road motor driver (Mr Savage) taking it from the station to the fishmongers in the railway Scammell. There was also a Sunday turn to Nottingham and back, while Birmingham and Wolverhampton were also on the rotas.

Basingstoke men had regular work on the Basingstoke to Reading stopping services. There was also a special working each day from Reading to Bramley for persons working at the CAD (Central Ammunition Depot). This was certainly operating when Dennis was a porter there during the Second World War and continued for a time after the war. At Bramley a CAD engine and coach (the latter of low profile and possibly a former Underground vehicle) met the train in the bay at the down platform ready to transport the workers to site.

When on the Reading turns, upon arrival Dennis's driver would leave him and expect the engine to be taken to the shed, watered, coaled (if necessary), turned, taken back to the station and attached to the train, all by a fireman on his own. It was quite a feat to read all the signals and discs even for the short distance to the shed and back, especially on 'foreign' territory. The driver would then miraculously reappear and take the train on – it was also expected that the footplate had been cleaned.

One day in No 2 platform at Reading, Dennis was using the pep-pipe to dampen down the coal dust and somehow became distracted. The next thing he remembered was a shout and holler from the platform – he looked up and saw that he had sprayed water all over a railway policemen. After the constable had established that it was an accident, all was well, but for a time Dennis had visions of being marched off to the police office on No 4 platform. Incidentally, right until the station remodelling, adjacent to the entrance to the station office was a very small square room that was the holding cell for miscreants, furnished with just a bench seat. It did not even have a window to the outside.

Another turn that came his way was on the prestige 'Cunarder' boat train from Waterloo to Southampton Docks, for which they were allocated a fairly new 'Class 5', No 73111. His driver at the time was known as a bit of a speed merchant but, despite having 'fourteen on', they made good time to Basingstoke, Worting and the summit of the line at Litchfield. At this point the driver opened up fully and speed increased rapidly, accompanied by the numerous rattles associated with these engines. Dennis takes up the story:

'We were doing close to 100mph when we spotted that the Winchester Junction distant was "on". For a few moments it was all very tense with a full brake application whilst for good measure I screwed the tender brake down. What had happened was the signalman had let the local from Alton out in front of us. Of course he was not to know what speed we had been making but fortunately the "home" came off as we approached, after which we could breathe again, even if it did mean following the local as far as Shawford before it could be turned off.'

It was a later fast run that gave Dennis what he would recall as his most memorable footplate trip ever. One morning he and his driver were told to relieve the crew of the 6.30am from Exeter and work it forward as the 9.13am to Waterloo. They relieved at the end of the platform to find that they had a 'Merchant Navy' in fine condition, and were soon off on the 48-mile journey. The schedule was a non-stop run due to the terminal at 10.08am, already one of the fastest steam times. Even so, Dennis and his driver gained no fewer than 8 minutes on the schedule, coming to a stand at exactly 10.00am, having taken just 47 minutes. 'We even had a clear run through Woking, which was unusual in those days as Portsmouth line trains were being given priority. I am not sure of the exact speed but reckon we were approaching 100mph at one point.' In 2016, with modern traction, the fastest schedule for the same route is 44 minutes, with most trains taking longer.

So far as the Southern Region was concerned, the various links at Basingstoke saw men working to Bournemouth, Salisbury, Portsmouth, Waterloo (semi-fast and fast services), Waterloo to Southampton Docks, Lymington, Bournemouth, Swanage, Weymouth, Feltham, Willesden (returning via Old Oak Common), Ludgershall and on trains to Amesbury and Bulford, which were usually in the hands of a Basingstoke 'Black Motor'. There was also an unusual turn to Sonning power station. Dennis also handled most locomotive types working on the Southern and some of the Western ones as well. His least favourite was the 'Lord Nelson' Class, due to the difficulty of firing the long firebox. On his first encounter with one of these, the driver saw that he was struggling to keep up steam and told him to move over while he was shown how to fire them. Not all drivers were so nice; indeed, some would not speak to their fireman for the whole shift.

'Merchant Navy' No 35011 awaits departure from Platform 3 at Basingstoke for Waterloo on an unreported date. The engine is ready and the crew look to be raring to go as well – possibly they were just keen to get home! The signals in the 'off' position are for the Reading line from Platform 4. Notice the operation of the signals themselves. No wires and rods here – instead the installation is controlled by the pneumatic system. Note the fireman's (?) headgear, a handkerchief or cloth, often worn by SR firemen in lieu of the more usual greasetop. Mike Upton recalls being told that it was less likely to slip off when firing and was thus more practical. Was this a practice solely restricted to main-line crews in the latter days of steam on the Southern, or maybe even a fashion statement by certain firemen? *Tony Woodforth collection*

An engine type Dennis did not like, mainly due to lack of familiarity and a 10-foot firebox, 'Lord Nelson' Class No 30857 *Lord Howe* stands at Basingstoke on 21 July 1962, albeit some years after Dennis had left the footplate. By this date the class was in severe decline, with just four of the original sixteen left in service. No 30857 would see out the summer service – just – but was taken out of traffic in September, the last two examples going for scrap the following month. As with depots elsewhere, a number of young firemen left the railway when light industry began to emerge in Basingstoke in the late fifties and early sixties. They (or their wives) were pleased to have a '9 to 5' job, with probably a canteen, and they would not have to wash and clean after each shift. The wives were certainly involved, working hard to do the washing necessary to keep overalls clean, for no self-respecting locoman would go to work looking scruffy and dirty. Dennis would religiously polish his shoes before each shift, although by the end of each turn they would not be in the same condition. No wonder it was difficult to keep up staffing levels at the various depots. The money too was poor compared with what could be earned outside, where there was less responsibility and no unsocial hours.

Railway life made those involved stick together. Mike Upton adds, 'I think we forget the importance of the roles of the wives in those days, not only the loneliness with husbands at work for long hours and unsocial hours but the need to keep quiet during the day when night shift men were sleeping. "Be quiet, Dad's asleep," was a regular admonishment in our house. Railway wives tended to mix with other railway wives as only they would understand the nuances of railway work and the issues that then arose. They often had to bring up the family more or less on their own, while the main two weeks holiday per year could be rostered at any time during the summer months and might not always be in August.' *Tony Woodforth collection*

On occasion Dennis was on the station pilot, which involved shunting Barton Mill siding as well as attaching/detaching vehicles from passenger trains. They were also there to take over from any failed engine on the down main line. On one particular day the down 'Bournemouth Belle' failed in Basingstoke station, the driver and fireman 'bailing out', stating that they would not take the train any further. Dennis and his driver were quickly commandeered, together with their rather scruffy 'U' Class 'Mogul' and, after the train engine had been detached, were rapidly attached to the Pullmans. Dennis recalls that due to the weight of the train and the condition of the engine, they struggled even to get away from the platform, but with plenty of sanding eventually managed to plod off, making slow time on the climb to the summit. What the passengers must have thought cannot be imagined, but already the telegraph wires were red hot and Eastleigh had found a more suitable replacement engine and a fresh crew ready to take over by the time they reached Southampton Central.

But for every prestige run like this, there was another that did not go so well, like the occasion they delayed a particular

Evidently the use of the Basingstoke station pilot for the 'Bournemouth Belle' was not unique, as a few years before his own experience No 31627 had been commandeered for the down train, although on this occasion there was evidently no replacement available at Southampton, so the 'U' is seen steaming west from the city with the 'next stop Bournemouth' – we hope! This particular incident took place on 6 August 1949. *Dennis Callender*

service in consequence of having a badly steaming 'S15'. It all started when they were told to work from Salisbury back to Basingstoke one evening with a very heavy coal train. By the time they had reached Grateley, Control had evidently had enough and the signalman indicated that they were to stop and reverse back into the up siding. This took quite some time, not helped by the state of the engine and the fact that they were now pushing the train uphill as the line here was otherwise on a down grade. When they had cleared the main line there was no steam left anyway, but they did notice the up 'ACE' sweep past hauled by main-line diesel No 10203. Because of the almost experimental nature of the new machine. its performance was being carefully monitored and for it to be held up was a serious crime. When they did reach Basingstoke and took the engine to the shed, the irate foreman wanted a report right away. They were subsequently saved by a fitter's report on the state of the engine, without which it would very likely have been a day's suspension without pay.

Again from Mike Upton: 'Timekeeping of trains was taken very seriously, even if there was no delay attribution in those days. Dad remembered taking over an inter-regional passenger train from a WR crew in the Reading area and passing Southcote Junction, a timing point, only a few minutes down. Dennis and his driver were only responsible for the service as far as Basingstoke but already by the time they went to book off shed at Basing, not some 30/40 minutes later, the shed foreman had a "please explain" ready for the driver. As I recall, Dad said the driver just wrote something along the lines of "engine badly clinkered up". No one challenged it and he heard no more of it. I think the supervision of trains by Control was tighter then than we in the computer age might think!'

Life on the railway was certainly not glamorous, but it did perhaps have its compensations as well. An example of this was when Dennis was on 'spare' and he might be sent on loan to Reading Southern. Here the duties would involve him on engines not normally seen at Basingstoke such as 'D' and 'E3' types, and routes that could take him to Feltham, Guildford, or more locally delivering wagons to Reading gas works or a trip to the sidings of the Huntley & Palmer biscuit factory. From the latter the company would send out a weekly van full of broken or damaged cakes and biscuits. These were available to railway staff at a reduced rate, a concession that continued right until the factory closed.

Another concession was during the Farnborough Air Show week. Basingstoke crews would assist in bringing the empty stock back from Farnborough to be serviced and stabled in the sidings at Barton Mill ready for the return. Each of these trains included a restaurant car, the crew of which would exchange food for hot water from the engine. Ascot race week was another occasional busy time, the coaching stock being worked via the now long-closed Frimley curve.

But times could also be tough. Working on the footplate in winter was bad. The cold would be there all the time, relieved only by the welcome warmth of the fire when the firebox doors were open, otherwise it was simply a case of huddling down in a corner to try and keep warm. Other times Dennis and his mate might stand for hours awaiting a path. This seemed to happen in summer, especially if they were on the local freight from Andover; such was the volume of traffic that if they were unable to get away before 1pm they might be stuck in the same position until 4pm or even later.

Another example of the type of situation Dennis could find himself in would be when, once nearly back to Basingstoke in charge of a long and mostly unfitted freight from Reading or Moreton Cutting, they might encounter the Bramley distant 'on' and the signalman leaning out the box window with his arms raised in a cross. This meant they were to draw forward, then reverse over the trailing crossover to the up line to wait for a following passenger train to pass. Such a move was galling to say the least, especially near the end of a long shift with an engine long out of shed and probably low on coal and water. A 14-hour shift with a poor-performing engine was not unusual, as even if they asked for relief they still had to get home. At the time the family lived not far from the railway, close to the Reading line near Basingstoke; if he was returning that way Dennis would give a special 'signal' on the whistle to let the family know he was at least on his way.

One far better day he does remember was 12 May 1955. Dennis was on the 4.30am carriage shunt with '700' No 30368. Halfway through the morning the foreman arrived to inform him that he was now a father, his son having been born that morning. Even so there was no chance of relief, and it was simply a question of completing the duty before he could visit his new family.

The same year (1955) had less happy memories, in particular the disastrous ASLEF strike from 29 May to 14 June. So far as Basingstoke was concerned it was almost a complete stoppage, with just two NUR firemen reporting for duty. Financially it was a terrible time for men with young families. Strike pay was just £1 10s per week, although the older footplate staff without young families helped by ensuring that those with young families received an extra 2s 6d per child. In the end it was just the drivers who received a pay rise – the firemen got nothing.

Dennis continued on the footplate until 1957, working various duties including often relieving engines and crews at Basingstoke on trains to and from the Western Region. In the normal course of events he would have been expected to have been made a driver in due course, but fate in the form of an accident at work resulted in a damaged back meant that his footplate days were over. The time spent on sick leave was tough, money was short and there was the fear he would not be fully fit again. As a fireman he could not expect concessions – the cab was no place for a 'passenger'.

But as per the oft-quoted phrase, 'When one door closes…', it was during this time that he learned of a vacancy as a lineman in the Signalling & Telegraph Department. He duly applied and was successful

Now his work involved maintaining the signalling, including the low-pressure pneumatic system in the area, together with the telephone network. (The term 'telegraph' was a throwback to earlier days, even though instruments of that name had long been superseded. It would not be until the mid-1960s and one of BR's many 'reorganisations' that the modern term 'telecoms' was substituted.) Dennis first worked with Jack Vickens, who had originally been employed by the firm that installed the pneumatic system and had then been taken on by the LSWR shortly afterwards to maintain the signalling – history would repeat itself here as well later… Jack was a real disciplinarian at work but a perfect gentlemen outside the job. Like many railwaymen he enjoyed his pint, especially on Saturday when they finished work at midday. It was then possible to trace his movements: Station Hotel, Railway Hotel, Rising Sun, after which he would wend his way home. After his formal retirement, Jack continued as a part-time lineman based in the old GWR station building at Basingstoke.

Jack retired soon after Dennis was transferred and was replaced by Jim Lucas. Jim was another example of a man who knew the job inside out, having been at Woking for a number of years. As a lineman, Dennis worked from 7.15am to 4.45pm with a 30-minute break, and took it in turns for after-hours call-outs. Later, the shift was changed, with one pair of men allocated a late turn, 1pm to 10pm, after which these same late-turn men were designated as 'on call' until the next early shift.

Dennis (assistant lineman) stands on the left with colleagues Des Painter (signalman, centre) and Frank Brooks (lineman) in about 1960. The line from Basingstoke to Southcote Junction was transferred to the Southern Region in 1950, hence Mortimer was a former GWR box complete with GWR fittings but now under SR maintenance. *Mike Upton collection*

If needed when 'on call', before the days of railway road transport, they were collected by a local taxi driver who had been alerted by Control. The driver used was a regular who seemed to work nights most of the time and who had also got to know where things were. An example was when there was a knock on the door in the middle of the night and the driver informed Dennis that there was a fault with the Overton down distant; strangely the driver knew where it was and even told Dennis where the nearest road access was. Once Dennis was on board, they collected his mate before going to the actual fault. The taxi driver always appeared to know who to collect first depending on the location of the problem; the S&T always worked as two-man gangs in those days.

With the railway between Basingstoke and Reading having come under the control of the Southern from 1950, and now included in the Woking maintenance district, Dennis would at times find himself at Mortimer or Bramley for maintenance. Mortimer was also where they played the occasional practical joke on the signalman, tying a detonator to the lever tail of the down distant lever (a hard pull due to the reverse curves); the consequent explosion when the lever was pulled would dislodge any amount of dust and debris, which rose though the lever frame quadrants in a cloud, accompanied by much coughing and spluttering by the signalman and probably some bad language too. It was the kind of practical joke now much frowned upon, but which was part of railway life in those days. Another time they attended a failure where the down rod of the up starting signal at Mortimer had broken, a rare event on GW signals. They took the two parts to a local blacksmith near the station who shut them together, and it was refitted, although Dennis had no idea how the bill was paid.

Weekend work could involve relaying and renewals including points and crossings. If they were due to work on replacing a turnout this was always scheduled for a Saturday night with the occupation being given up by 9am – there was no overrunning in those days. The Permanent Way Department was known to be able to undertake 1 mile of hand relaying over a Saturday night.

During the bad winter of 1963, Dennis recalled being called out two or even three times in one night. On one occasion this was when all electric power had been lost at each of the automatic signals between Basingstoke and Farnborough, and the most effective cure was to replace the dry cell batteries at each. Not surprisingly this would have been far too much weight for two men to carry, so the batteries were loaded on to the footplate of a commandeered engine and the requisite number thrown off at each signal as they passed. Dennis and his mate then had the unenviable task of walking back along the complete length in the dark installing the batteries as necessary. He recalls, 'It was so cold when we finished, we lit a fire under the railway arch at Old Basing just to try and keep warm.'

Heavy snow and strong winds could also bring down the telegraph wires, which would mean walking sometimes miles carrying ladders. Two of them might regularly cycle along the cess by the side of the rails with a long ladder strung between them; one slip and they would have ended up either on the ballast or down the embankment, but it rarely seemed to happen. One night it did at Burghfield on the Reading line. Rather than carry the railway ladder some distance, they had the bright idea of asking a local farmer if he could help as his farm was close to the railway. The farmer agreed but only on the condition that they repair his electric cooker first. They succeeded with the cooker but the ladder was enormous and it was a work of art trying to get it positioned between the line wires.

Spares for the GWR fittings on the Reading line meant a trip to the signal works at Caversham Road, Reading. On one occasion they ordered a complete set of mechanical gate fittings for the level crossing at Bramley. These duly arrived in a wagon and were left in the old goods yard siding. Southern spares were obtained from Woking. Every Thursday, a man from each depot would go to Woking by train and bring back all the stores needed. These were then loaded into the guard's van, including paraffin, and deposited at the station nearest each depot. This was of course before the days of road transport, so everything was moved by train.

Maintenance to a point motor (the trailing end of crossover 16, up relief to up main) at Hook in 1960. Left to right the men are Dennis Upton, Frank Brooks and Davis (Bill) Johnson. *Mike Upton collection*

Dennis was also involved in dealing with the consequences of any number of minor derailments; wherever possible these were dealt with locally without 'top brass' becoming involved. One regular problem was when a train arrived from Reading and ran into No 5 platform. The engine could only be released through a mechanical ground frame to reach what was known as No 6 road and therefore run round its train. Operation of this ground frame was the responsibility of the shunters, but they had a habit of failing to pull the points fully over and the result would be bent rodding. There was always a spare drive rod hanging up under 'C' box for such occurrences. During failures or incidents, if absolutely necessary, a special train service was introduced with single-line working, but the public was always the priority and there were no replacement buses.

To show what work had been carried out locally, there was a daily occurrence book kept under each signal box. Here the men would record what had been carried out, the book being periodically inspected by the signal engineer who would countersign the entries. Some men might try and falsify work, but it was a risky procedure. The local inspector was Charlie Pitt, a former army major, very strict but fair and who never missed a trick. No one ever succeeded in pulling the wool over Charlie's eyes. If the men were working on a Sunday it was not unknown for Charlie to turn up on site with his wife in his car – just to check that no one had gone home early.

In 1965/66, in connection with the Bournemouth electrification, plans were drawn up for the replacement of the mechanical signalling – the era of the push-button had arrived, Messrs Westinghouse and Elliot Automation being the main contractors. The new signalling was operational in January 1967, perhaps not unexpectedly with a few teething troubles, but not many. The men were transferred to the new system with no training; they simply had to learn as they went along. As Dennis puts it, '…even the signal engineer's department had not got a clue.' Here, though, history would indeed repeat itself, as the Westinghouse designer Derek Hotchkiss was offered the job of signal engineer to look after the new installations. Via Derek there came much help in explaining Westinghouse Mark 1 interlocking, which was much appreciated. Dennis would never forget the help given him by Derek. Otherwise the men learned the hard way how to rectify failures and the easy way of unlocking relays that had stuck the wrong way round. Dennis continues, 'What we did may have been frowned upon by senior management, but they did not have an alternative, so provided they were not present, a blind eye was turned. We always made sure there were no traffic movements outside.'

One advantage of the new signalling was that the technicians (as they were now called) had their own transport, which saved a lot of walking. Dennis could not drive, so the railway paid for his driving lessons. Other improvements were with messing, as they were now attached to the main building. Another change was that there was now a proper night shift, meaning that someone was quickly on hand in the event of a problem. Compared with the past, the whole area was now controlled by just two signalmen and two S&T men on each shift.

One event involving Dennis that could have spelled the end of not just his career but also his life occurred in the long hot summer of 1976. Together with his mate he was attending a failure near the site of what had been Silchester level crossing on the Basingstoke to Reading line. It was a hot Friday evening and the rails had already been subjected to the daytime heat. Unbeknown to all, a buckle occurred in the rails just as a northbound Freightliner was travelling over it at around 70mph. Fortunately most of the train managed to pass over the damaged track, but the rear portion was derailed and remained coupled. Dennis was already standing by the trackside waiting for the train to pass when he became aware of ballast and sleepers flying in all directions. It was time for immediate action and he dived into the ditch alongside the line, hoping that the wagons would not topple over. He admits that he was never so scared in all his life. Fortunately the train did remain upright,

Pneumatic signals at Fleet (up main and up relief starting) just before their replacement. These LSWR lower-quadrant arms had been in position since installation, although missing is the post and arm that had once existed between the two to control a crossover from the relief to the main. The short-post upper-quadrant rail-built signal on the right controlled the exit from the down sidings. *Tony Woodforth collection*

The morning after the night before. The changeover from mechanical to colour light signals took place on 20 November 1966, and this was the scene on the morning of the 21st, the semaphore arms removed and the colour light signal – well one at least – displaying for the first time. *Tony Woodforth collection*

The new panel at Basingstoke. Just above the hand of the operator (believed to be a representative from the manufacturer) it is possible to identify the station platforms. *Noodle Books collection*

but it took a mile and a half to stop, damaging the same amount of permanent way. It transpired that both Dennis and his mate had taken the same course of action, but not knowing if the other was safe. Although severely shaken, fortunately both were unhurt. On this occasion, buses were resorted to, but train services had been restored by lunchtime on Saturday. A report in the local *Basingstoke Gazette* commented that a British Rail spokesman 'would neither confirm nor deny that the derailment had been caused by the buckling of lines due to the record-breaking weekend temperatures.'

Dennis remained on the railway, continuing with the S&T Department until his retirement, not only a life-long railwayman but also an enthusiast throughout. His son Mike Upton has also worked in railway engineering throughout his own career, and his grandson works for a signalling contractor.

The last words are perhaps best left to Mike Upton: 'I was with Dad one day while he and Frank were working on a semaphore gantry on the high embankment above the village of Old Basing. A lady from a house at the bottom of the bank saw me and wanted to know what I was doing there. Dad appeared and told her I was with him and no more was said. To think I was left to walk around – I was told not to go on the tracks, while trains thundered along the four-track railway – no wonder I was hooked! I was especially fond of the Bulleids in their original form; to me they looked so modern, stylish and different from the usual locos; from those times I was smitten by Mr Bulleid's "mercurial maidens" as I once saw them described. But then I did not have to maintain them.

'I clearly remember as a young boy a feeling of awe when entering a signal box: first there was a mix of smells, lino polish,

oil, maybe a coal fire and that indefinable smell of the wiring used in boxes and interlockings. Then the quietly confident and assured way the signalman went about his duties: bells codes, block instruments to work, a telephone query about an additional train or one running out of course, gossip on the box-to-box phone… Levers effortlessly pulled, and when I was given the offer to pull one, oh how hard it was to pull them – a gentle laugh as the signalman then threw it with one hand. "It's the knack, you know, boy, the knack." Strong tea as well, but perhaps not always – one signalman at Bramley was famous for getting many cups out of one teapot, forever topping it up with hot water!

'Dad's friend Jack Hunt at Bramley lived just down the road from the station and when on early turn his wife would bring his cooked breakfast up the road on a covered plate, and he would meet her at the door of the box. There were occasional moans about the cleaning not being done properly, each of the regular men having set things to clean; with so many windows, for instance, not everyone was thorough. I never heard bad language – these were proud, assured men who carried out what we now refer to as "safety critical" duties without fuss and with a deep sense of responsibility and proficiency. Oh, and always grumbles about the relief signalman not cleaning or doing things properly. "Relief men" were also paid a special rate, and this was always a bone of contention with the regulars. One of the porters at Bramley

Dennis recalled that following the incident the assistant station manager from Basingstoke was on site very quickly, with the priority to get traffic moving. This was achieved through single-line working, with dead-slow and watchful passage past the actual derailment. It is believed that this continued until the derailment was cleared and both lines were again available for traffic.

Rail track twister

THE main Reading to Basingstoke freight line was blocked for nearly ten hours on Saturday morning when a goods train was derailed near Silchester.

The front wagon of a Reading bound freight train was derailed just seconds after pulling out of Bramley Station.

The wagon jumped the lines and the train carried on – wrecking more than a mile and a half of track.

Dozens of freight and passenger trains were subjected to lengthy delays and several buses were comandeered to ferry stranded rail travellers to their destinations.

Repair crews worked through the early hours of Saturday morning to clear the blocked line and by lunchtime train services were operating normally.

A spokesman for British Rail said an internal investigation was to be carried out into the cause of the derailment.

The spokesman would neither confirm nor deny that the derailment had been caused by the buckling of lines due to the record-breaking weekend temperatures.

Modern-day (well, MAS-era) maintenance at Basingstoke, but still on air points. Dennis (left) is oiling on a cold winter morning, with his colleague Frank Brooks. The location is the London end of Platform 4 (the up local line) with the Reading bay to the right of the fence, circa 1979. By this time there had been a change in job titles; instead of 'assistant lineman', Dennis was now a 'technician', and Frank, who had previously been graded 'lineman', was now 'senior technician'. This had come about following a 'Pay and Grading' review that was an attempt to put some structure into the technician grades by requiring attendance (and successful results) at various training courses.

Mike Upton comments: 'The air points that were left after rationalisation in Basingstoke station and immediate area (but not, I think, at Winchfield or Farnborough, which were converted to electrical) were all re-controlled from the new PSB interlocking in 1965. From that date into at least the 1980s there was a piecemeal approach to replacing air-operated points with rail-mounted clamp locks, although some point machines may have been used. The local men thought, maybe a little unfairly, that the managers/supervisors did not understand air so wanted it replaced, but more likely the equipment was life-expired and I do recall that usable spares became a problem towards the end. The problem of air leakage in all the pipework around the station area was also becoming quite serious towards the end, but to be fair it had been there rather a long time. The "pump house", as it was known, containing both compressor and a large reservoir, was on the up side between the underbridge by the Holy Ghost Ruins and the start of the station buildings on Platform 4, a single-storey brick building, flat-roofed, very SR in appearance. I went in there once and by then the compressor was run by an immaculately kept diesel engine maintained by the ODM (Outdoor Machinery Department) based at Eastleigh. I think before that it may have been operated by a small steam engine, but I am not sure.' *Andy French*

A location Dennis would have known well was Basingstoke 'B', which controlled the west end of the station layout until MAS took over. The large tank at the end was for the pneumatic operation of the points and signals, which also explains why there is no point rodding and signal wires at the base of the box. Basingstoke 'B' must have been a comfy working environment with no draughts coming up through the floor.

Moving on to the Reading line for a moment, during Dennis's time on the footplate one of the regular signalmen, Jack Hunt at Bramley, became a lifelong friend. Jack was a dyed-in-the-wool GWR man and did not much like working for the Southern. His father had been station master at Hermitage. When Basingstoke panel came into being, Jack was very disparaging about the emergency block bell provided for communication in the event of a failure of the train describer. This he referred to as being 'like a village tea shop bell', a far cry from the solid tones of the GWR block bells. If Jack was on duty at Bramley when Dennis was on the footplate, they could be sure of a can of hot water or tea and maybe a warm by the signal box fire if the turn allowed, especially reviving on a cold winter's morning when running tender-first, something that happened more often than is appreciated and was caused by having no time to run to shed and turn. Mike Upton recalls that he could never remember a signalman being called 'bobby', even from his youngest days when accompanying his father to work. 'Mum suffered from ill health and, having no means of looking after me on school holidays, I went to work with father.' It was always a respectful 'Good morning, officer', before reverting to the signalman's first name.

also did the lampman's duties, and was legendary for not trimming the lamps. Not surprisingly, he gained the nickname "Sooty" (an oil lamp will quickly produce soot if the wick is not correctly trimmed). Then there was the local permanent way gang trimming the banks with enormous scythes, sharpened on equally huge circular grinding stones at each P-way hut, each man given a length of bank to trim paced out by the ganger. No one would offer to help another; whoever had finished would simply watch until all had finished.

'As a young lad I recall the one piece of advice given by an old ganger: 'Don't sit on the rail, boy, you will get piles.' Nothing about getting run down by a train! Perhaps that was why some of these men carried a little piece of old sacking to put on the rail top before sitting down prior to having a rest or even a bite to eat. One old boy in the gang had a large raw onion and a bottle of cold tea every day for lunch – really...'

Hither Green Firebox Collapse

The incidence of a boiler explosion or firebox collapse on Britain's railways was fortunately a rare occurrence – certainly in the 20th century. Earlier times might well be considered to have been slightly different, but with higher pressures and more experience, engineers, designers, maintenance staff and crews each began to appreciate that they had their own part to play in ensuring that pressurised steam stayed exactly where it was intended – inside the boiler and under control.

That is not to say that there were not some failures, varying from the catastrophic to the less so, and due to a myriad of causes. Away from the Southern we can report that the last case of a firebox collapse on British Railways, caused by lack of water, took place at Bletchley on 24 January 1962. Before that, there were several others including the well-known incident involving the American 'S160' engine at Honeybourne during the Second World War when the crew were misled by the indication of the water gauge.*

So far as the Southern Railway (and others) was concerned it would be fair to say that there were probably few locomotive crews who had not come close to uncovering the crown of the firebox at some time during their careers and often through no fault of their own. Fortunately, in 99.9% of cases some skilful handling resolved the situation, perhaps at the expense of loss of time and/or a stop for a 'blow-up'. It would take a very foolish crew to continue pushing their engine beyond what they knew were the safe limits of working. Even so, as a safeguard, fusible plugs were fitted to the roof of the firebox, the lead core of which would melt, so dousing the fire with water if the lead was subjected to excess heat. Otherwise the resultant explosive effect of hot water spraying into the firebox could well have its own volatile consequences. Also to be considered was the situation whereby the top of the firebox, and in particular the stays, had been weakened through prolonged exposure to similar excess heat. The strength and integrity of the stays would thus be gradually diminished, although this would normally be expected to be picked up during boiler examinations. It is exactly such a case with which we now concern ourselves.

* Other similar firebox problems occurred on 'Lord Nelson' No 854 on 23 April 1945 (see 'SW' issue 17), and at Bevois Park near Southampton on 6 April 1949, this time involving 'E4' No 2557.

No 1572 has literally blown itself off the track at Hither Green on 15 October 1947. The engine had been placed on a track outside the shed and at 9.15am the driver and fireman started to prepare it for what should have been the 10.00am freight to Old Oak Common. *Southern Railway*

It was fortunate that the incident occurred outside the shed, for had it taken place inside there would certainly have been the chance of more damage/injury within a confined space. Following the incident, the 'Mogul' behind was hemmed in until No 1572 was re-railed. The collapse occurred just before 10.00am when both men were on the footplate. Not surprisingly, both were burned and scalded, the fireman the more so because he was blown off the footplate. *Southern Railway*

Unfortunately, what a locomotive crew had no control over was when either poor, or at worst no, maintenance/inspection rendered a boiler dangerous (and in what follows, for 'boiler' please read the complete assembly meaning boiler *and/or* firebox). This is exactly what took place when the firebox of 'C' Class 0-6-0 No 1572 (boiler No 81) collapsed at Hither Green on the morning of 15 October 1947.

At that time, when incidents such as this occurred, they were subject to an internal railway enquiry, this one being held at Ashford Works on Tuesday 28 October 1947, Ashford being the works responsible for maintenance of the boiler in question. Three men were present to try and establish the facts: Mr M. S. Hatchell (in the chair), Mr J. E. Bell, and Mr L. J. Granshaw. It is believed that Mr Hatchell was the Ashford Works Manager, and while the position held by Mr Bell is not reported, Mr Granshaw was the Brighton Works Manager.

The report, which runs to nine typed sides, consists of a transcript of questions and answers between the three men mentioned above and initially two others, Messrs Rogers and Nicholls from the Motive Power Department.

At the very start we also find the cause of the incident, failure of the firebox roof stays. We also learn that an apparent lack of communication had occurred, the roof stays having been at least 'partially cleaned', after which the whole boiler was examined by an Assistant Foreman. This man was, however,

acting as a relief for the normal individual, who was on leave. When the regular man returned he would have been responsible for informing the chargeman as to what work was required. There was another written record referred to – see the next paragraph – but not with the existing report papers, confirming that the stays did require renewing, but for whatever reason this was not passed on and in consequence the work was not carried out. The names of the Assistant Foreman involved are given in the report, but have purposely been withheld here.

Referring to the additional report, the questioning of Messrs Rogers and Nichols begins: 'In the report of your enquiry, reference is made to the examination of stays. Do you refer to all stays, roof stays, water space stays, etc?'

There followed what might well be described as a 'cross-examination', which continued for 3½ pages – twenty-eight separate questions, variously asked by the three senior men present.

The questions centred around procedure, and it was immediately apparent that the line of enquiry was concentrating upon works rather than shed procedure when it came to the previous examination, marking of, and undertaking necessary boiler repairs. As an example:

Mr Hatchell: 'If the stays are suspected are they marked off?'

Answer (not specified by whom): 'If it so happens that there is an element of doubt, we put down "For stay examination". If

The force of the blast would have been primarily downwards, sufficient to lift up then set down the engine, and, to a lesser extent, forward and back. That going forward had been enough to sling open the smokebox door with much force. *Southern Railway*

they are bad we say "Roof stays renewing".'

The questioning continued in similar vein, during which time it emerged that boiler No 81 had received a works repair in 1944. (By inference the same boiler was on the same engine at the time.) The works report at that time indicated 'Roof stays renewing'.

This last comment is important, for it emerged that in addition other firebox work was also considered necessary. However, we now come to the damning part of the evidence, for while there was a record of the 'other' firebox work having been carried out, that relative to the roof stays seems to have simply been omitted.

Grate and ashpan material is deposited on the sleepers. The track and sleepers have also suffered. Re-railing would have been carried out by the shed breakdown gang, possibly on call-out. Unfortunately they would not qualify for call-out payment as the incident was well within shed limits. *Both Southern Railway*

A short time later the paperwork refers to the issue of hydraulic and steam testing after repair, undertaken at 25% + 10lb over the normal working pressure for the hydraulic, and a lesser 10lb over normal working pressure for the subsequent steam test.

The questioning then moved to the two Assistant Foremen involved, where it was pointed out that the relieving man was from the Erecting Shop. Thirty-two questions and answers were recorded, one of these providing the information that the firebox itself was only six years old and 'should not have been in such a bad condition'. The respondent continued, 'You do find on "C" Class boilers the roof stays go rapidly sometimes – that is why you examine all of them.' It was noted that an NUR representative was also present during the questioning of one of the men.

No time was given for the duration of the questioning and the paperwork does not give a formal conclusion, although having read the detail, much of which is repetitive and so unnecessary to repeat here, it is possible to surmise what the final result was.

Messrs Hatchell, Bell and Granshaw were attempting to establish what sort of boiler examinations were taking place, who was responsible for them and, most importantly, that if work was noted as being required, who was responsible for carrying it out. The first two were fairly clear-cut – it was the connection between the second and third where the weak link existed. The Assistant Foreman would have a personal book in which he entered a record of work needing to be carried out, the requisite information then being communicated verbally to the chargehand who was responsible for seeing that the actual work was carried out. Clearly the problems on No 1572 had been noted, but somewhere along the line either the stand-in Assistant Foreman or the normal man had failed to pass on the message. Whatever, the result was the explosion on No 1572, but also an immediate change of procedure, which was already in place by 28 October, whereby a 'paper trail' would now exist. Two copies of the 'work required' sheet were now being made out, one of which would be given to the chargehand and the other retained and subsequently initialled to confirm that the work had been completed.

No 1572 might therefore have been said to have been an accident waiting to happen. It was only down to the fortitude of the men who had worked her before that the incident had not occurred earlier.

...where once there had been a set of firebox doors... The collapsed firebox top may be seen within, together with numerous missing and broken stays. It has not been possible to trace where No 1572 was repaired after the incident, although again Ashford would appear to be the most likely. *Southern Railway*

One question not answered was whether any responsibility was passed to the boiler examiner at Hither Green depot. There is no mention of this within the paperwork, although to examine the stays in what was the boiler space was certainly not an easy operation, but was a regular part of the servicing procedure, certainly during times of boiler wash-out. On the fateful morning the crew would have been slowly building up steam pressure preparatory to taking their booked train – that is, until the pressure just got too great for the firebox to withstand. As has been seen, the force of the explosion was sufficient to lift the engine bodily, 44½ tons excluding tender, and deposit it alongside where it had been standing. Under the circumstances anyone nearby might well have been forgiven for momentarily believing the Blitz had started all over again.

For the moment at least there would appear to be nothing else to say concerning No 1572, Board of Trade reports and national newspapers having failed to reveal any reference to the incident. It was perhaps extremely fortunate that No 1572 had not been working a train at the time. The engine, however, would be repaired and soldier on, although it was destined to be one of the early members of the type to be withdrawn, by now as BR No 31572, in February 1954.

This unusual view needs some explanation as to its orientation. The vertical bars at the top are the grate, and the firehole door is apparent. The curved plate is the collapsed arch pulled away from the throat plate by the force of the explosion; it is this that is seen in the previous image – through the open gap where the firehole doors should be. The copper firebox's flat crown was carried by eight longitudinal roof girders and held in place with 112 mild steel 1-inch stays. It was these stays that had given way due to severe corrosion, a fact not picked up due to procedural lapses at Ashford*. *Southern Railway*

* Reference also *Locomotive Boiler Explosions* by C. H. Hewison (David & Charles, 1983)

In the Glasshouse
Southern Railway Signal Box Design, 1936-1946

The exterior of the signal box at Surbiton, complete with rounded corners and plate glass. The uninterrupted glass area differed from the Southampton and Millbrook examples, which had two glazing bars per window. Note that the roof is only rounded at the front corners; this was the general practice when there was no track at the rear of the box, otherwise all four corners were rounded. But of course there were also exceptions – Bognor, for example, had no track at the rear but also had rounded corners! *Westinghouse*

The Southern Railway 'glasshouse' or 'Odeon' type of signal box must rank among the most striking of all signal box designs – bar none. What became the developed design was first seen in 1936, although similar-style structures had already been introduced in June 1935 at both Southampton Central and Millbrook, commensurate with the quadrupling of the line between these two points at that time. By 1936 the design had been modified to include rounded corners and plate glass, the first of the new boxes in this style being commissioned at Surbiton in 1936.

By 1940 more than a dozen boxes of the type had been constructed, and while we are concerned here with the 'glasshouse' design having extensions or 'wings' on either side, it should be mentioned that some boxes of similar style (but without the ground floor extensions) were also provided, Deal and Redhill No 1 being examples. In such cases all the requisite locking and other equipment could be adequately accommodated beneath the main structure without the need for a separate relay room and/or ancillary accommodation – usually for the local S&T linemen.

Woking received its new box in 1937, located at the west end of the station between the up and down running lines. At the time of writing, 2016, it remains in situ. The year 1938 was clearly a busy time for the 'new works' section of the S&T Department, with several of the new type opened. Among them were Dorking North (15 March 1938), Arundel (27 March 1938), Horsham (24 April 1938), Templecombe (15 May 1938), Bognor

The interior of Surbiton, with its Westinghouse 'A2' frame of 52 levers at 4-inch centres. A point to note is that this was a rearward-facing frame, the idea being that the signalman would therefore have an uninterrupted view of passing trains. This also became standard practice for the Southern Railway. Possibly (but not confirmed), Southampton may have been the first occasion when the rearward-facing frame was used; it could not have been Millbrook as here there were running lines passing each side of the box. While stating that the rearwards-facing frame was adopted as standard, many boxes would survive until closure without this feature. In this view a number of short-handle levers will be noted; these operated signals, motor points or other equipment that was not mechanically worked, the short lever in reality little more than a switch and as such a reminder to the signalman that little effort would be required.
Westinghouse

The notice issued for the commissioning of the new box at Surbiton in 1936.

SOUTHERN RAILWAY.

Signal Instruction No. 21, 1936.

Instructions to all concerned as to

INTRODUCTION OF COLOUR LIGHT SIGNALS BETWEEN MALDEN AND HAMPTON COURT JUNCTION

(In place of existing semaphore running signals)

AND

BRINGING INTO USE NEW SIGNAL BOXES AND ABOLITION OF EXISTING SIGNAL BOXES AT SURBITON AND HAMPTON COURT JUNCTION;

ALSO

SLEWING OF DOWN LOCAL LINE AT SURBITON

ON SUNDAY, 28th JUNE, 1936.

Rules 77, 78, 79 and 80 to be observed. Drivers to keep a good look-out for hand signals.

Commencing at 12.5 a.m. on Sunday, 28th June, colour light signals will be installed between Malden and Hampton Court Junction in place of existing semaphore running signals.

A new signal box will be provided on the up side at Surbiton, 118 yards west of the station, and the existing signal box will be abolished.

A new signal box will be provided at Hampton Court Junction, adjacent to the existing signal box which will be abolished.

The down local line at Surbiton will be slewed to the left in the direction of travel commencing at a point 315 yards east of the station to a point 108 yards west of the station and will, in future, be served by the platform on the right-hand side.

The existing facing connection from up local to up through line, operated from Marsh Lane box, will be abolished, and a new facing connection (No. 14) from up local to up through line, to be operated from Surbiton box, will be provided 488 yards east of that box.

A new "limit of shunt" indicator will be provided between the down local and down through lines at Surbiton 418 yards east of the signal box and the indicator must not be passed in connection with shunting movements back on the down local line.

The two ground signals west of Surbiton box controlling movements from down local line and down siding to up local or up through line will, in future, also apply back on down local line as far as the "limit of shunt" indicator.

A diagram showing the altered signalling is attached to this notice, the colour light running signals being prefixed by letters to denote from which box the signals are worked, as follows:—

Prefix Letters.	Signal Box.
M.L.	Marsh Lane.
W.N.	Surbiton.
W.P.	Hampton Court Junction.

A plate bearing the prefix letters and the number of the signal will be fixed to each signal post carrying running signals.

Automatic signals are prefixed by the letters W.A. and are identified by a white plate with a horizontal black band.

Semi-automatic signals are prefixed by the letters denoting the signal box from which they can be controlled and are identified by a white plate bearing the word "SEMI" above a horizontal black band.

Marsh Lane box will be switched out of circuit for certain periods and during the time this signal box is closed the running signals will work automatically.

2

The colour light running signals will show four or three aspects and will be known as automatic, semi-automatic, or controlled signals, viz.:—

Automatic signals are those which are not worked from a signal box and are controlled by track circuit only.

Semi-automatic signals are those which are controlled from one or more signal boxes when such boxes are open, in addition to being controlled by track circuit, but which, when the boxes are closed, work automatically and are then controlled by track circuit only.

Controlled signals are those which are always controlled from a signal box and are also controlled by track circuit.

The auxiliary colour light running signal (W.N. 44) at Surbiton will normally show no light and a yellow aspect will be shown for movements from down local line to down siding.

The lights of the four-aspect running signals will be arranged as shown on the diagram and not as appearing on page 4 of the General Appendix to the Working Time Tables.

The aspects of the colour light running signals will be the same by day as by night.

Colour light running signals will be fitted with small side lights repeating the aspects exhibited by the signals to assist Drivers of trains drawn close up to such signals.

Back lights will not be provided in any of the colour light running signals.

The height of the centre of the red light of the colour light running signals will vary between 10 and 18 feet above rail level.

Track circuits have been installed throughout the area covered by the colour light signals and all colour light running signals and certain shunt signals at Surbiton will be controlled by the track circuits.

Colour light running signals are replaced to Danger after the engine has passed a distance varying from 15 to 233 yards beyond the signal.

"P" (proceed) signs will be provided at certain automatic signals, as indicated on the diagram, for use in accordance with the Instructions under the heading "Passing signals at Danger" on pages 5 and 6 of the Supplement dated 4th March, 1936, to the book of Instructions for the information of Drivers, Firemen and Guards.

The Instructions under the following headings appearing in Signal Instruction No. 18, 1936, will apply as between Malden and Hampton Court Junction.

JUNCTION INDICATORS.
FAILURE OF SIDE LIGHT.
TELEPHONES.
SIGNALLING IN FOGGY WEATHER OR DURING FALLING SNOW.
SWITCHES FOR PLACING SIGNALS AT DANGER.

On completion of the work shown herein the alterations in and additions to the book of Instructions to Drivers, Firemen and Guards, dated 31st March, 1935, contained in the supplement dated 4th March, 1936, will operate between Malden and Hampton Court Junction.

F. BUSHROD,
Superintendent of Operation.

Waterloo Station.
8th June, 1936.

(R. 55497.)

Waterlow & Sons Limited, London Wall, London.

Regis (29 March 1938), and Ascot 'B' (16 October 1938). Templecombe was the furthest west the design would be seen and was also platform-mounted. Following rationalisation of resources at Templecombe following closure of the S&D and the singling of the former LSWR main line to the west around the same time, the lever frame was considerably shortened, the vacant space taking on a new use as the station booking office.

While the Second World War generally brought to an understandable stop any further new builds of the type, one was commissioned at Richmond Junction on 28 January 1940, followed by Redhill No 1 on 15 June 1941. After this there was a gap of several years before a more modest programme was instigated, starting with Portsmouth Harbour on 1 June 1946, to be followed shortly after by Blackfriars Junction on 11 August, both of these being permanent replacements for infrastructure damaged during the war. Later in 1947 came Twickenham West (19 January) and Wimbledon East on 29 February 1948. This brought the total of the type to eighteen.

After 1950 the Southern Region modified the design with variations to the roof and windows. A further fourteen boxes were built to this modified type up to 1955, after which replacement structures were to a variety of designs involving conventional brick, an 'over-sailing' operating floor above a locking/relay room, or using precast concrete panels.

Dorking North, opened 15 March 1938, is recorded here in July of that year. A point to note is the style and position of the wording, which was unaltered into BR days. (Was the name temporarily removed to hamper a potential invader during the war?) Notwithstanding the rails behind the box, there are no rounded corners to the rear of the roof. At the time of opening the same type of lever frame was provided as at Surbiton, but slightly reduced at 44 levers. *Southern Railway*

Opposite top: **The brand-new box at Arundel (27 March 1938). Aesthetically the rectangular extensions at each end probably blend better with the square corners to the rear of the roof. Compared with Dorking North, the ground floor extensions are also shorter. 'Health & Safety' is also apparent with the guard rails protecting the exit from the ground floor doors towards the running line.** *Southern Railway*

Bottom: **Several decades later, the exterior is seen here after privatisation. Externally the structure remains much as built but with some obvious additions, including the chimney. (Can we count the hole in the brickwork of the end wall as an 'addition'?) Access to the operating area was via an internal set of stairs at the near end.** *Railtrack*

The interior of Arundel, having been converted from its original mechanical status. The exterior chimney would appear to be redundant. *Railtrack*

Opposite top: This later view of Bognor Regis incorporates a colour light distant below the starting signal. Again it has a rearward-facing frame, with rounded rear corners to the roof despite there being no track behind. *Southern Railway*

Bottom: Horsham was provided with a 90-lever frame. The Victorian water tower of the engine shed appears somewhat incongruous with the Art Deco design of the signal box. Once again a variation in size and position of the lower windows will be noted. Whether the variation in such external detail was warranted, or the architect was simply playing with aesthetics, is not certain. *Southern Railway*

Ascot week in June 1938 afforded an opportunity for one intrepid individual to record progress on the new 'glasshouse' box then under construction at the station. Ascot 'B', as it would be known, was commissioned on 16 October 1938 and again displays a variation in design, apparently without any windows towards the running line.

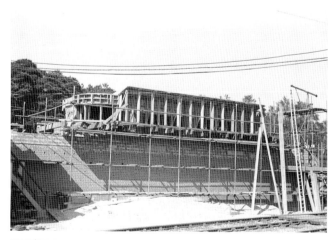

Strood Junction (29 January 1939) was opened at the same time as the similar Strood Tunnel box. Here at the junction we have yet another variant in design: no windows in the lower floor (as per Ascot), the centre pillar between the end windows replaced by another pane of glass, and, most obvious, the raised operating area. The whole combines to give a more practical design for the location, even if it is certainly more austere and subjectively less pleasing to the eye. (Woking was similar.) With running lines to front and rear, the obvious question might be where to place the lever frame, although this would be sited so as to afford maximum view to the principal route. One unanswered question is, what were working conditions like in extremes of weather? Certainly signal boxes generally created an environment that could be cold in winter, due to draughts coming up from the necessary holes at the base, where rodding and wires emerged, but also extremely hot in summer thanks to the amount of glass – curtains were *not* permitted! (Windows were often blacked out during the Second World War to leave just a small viewing slit.) From the number of windows open here, we may assume that it is a warm environment. *E. R. Wethersett*

An end-on view of Swanley box, which was built at the country end of the station and opened in April/July 1939. This design of signal box, regardless of whether there were ground floor extensions, is given Signalling Record Society classification 'SR-13'.

Fifty Years On
Counting Down to July 2017
Part 2, Winter 1966/67

The photographs of Jim Seddon, by Andrea Durrant

Above: With the exception of the Pullman 'Bournemouth Belle' and certain boat trains, most services operating on the Bournemouth line were anonymous, both headboards and carriage roof boards rapidly becoming a thing of the past. We have to thank Jim for noting specific workings such as this one of the morning up 'Royal Wessex', usually booked for a 'Merchant Navy' but instead seen behind 'West Country' No 34013 *Okehampton*, approaching Byfleet & New Haw on Friday 25 November 1966. Unusually too for the period, the engine retains its nameplate and crest. The first coach is a green Mk 2 all 1st, one of several built at Eastleigh and outshopped in Southern green.

Opposite top: As if to emphasise the earlier comment about the anonymity of Bournemouth-line services at the time, this is in fact a Southampton Docks to Waterloo 'Ocean Liner' special behind No 73118 (formerly *King Leodegrance*) at the same location and noted by Jim as passing '30 minutes later'. A subtle clue as to the type of train might be the presence of the two luggage vans at the front. Obviously a mixed rake is being used, for the fourth vehicle is another BR Mk 2 1st Class coach.

Bottom: When a rebuilt 'Bulleid' was travelling at speed, a vacuum would develop around the top of the smokebox ahead of the chimney, causing steam to circulate in this area before being caught by the blast and dispersed. This is shown to good effect on No 34108 *Wincanton*, recorded passing Byfleet & New Haw on 30 December 1966, in charge of the 07.30 Weymouth to Waterloo train. Jim notes that at this time the surviving Bulleid engines were averaging 6,000 miles a month, a reasonable figure bearing in mind that this includes a number doubtless doing much more, while others in run-down condition were far short of this figure.

A clean No 35012 *United States Lines* passes Vauxhall with the 10.30 Waterloo to Bournemouth train on 9 February 1967. The leaking steam from the front end is indicative of a piston gland, while according to *The Book of the Merchant Navies* withdrawal in April 1967 was due to a leaking boiler barrel joint. Just visible on the end of the first vehicle (a Mk 1) is a set number, '156', although possibly this may not apply any longer as it would be unlikely for vehicles in different liveries to be combined in a numbered set.

Opposite top: No 34057 *Biggin Hill* was possibly one of those that was so restricted, but is seen here at Vauxhall on a very cold December day in 1966 with the Saturdays-only 12.30 local from Waterloo to Basingstoke. Allocated to Salisbury, the white embellishments indicate recent railtour use, while externally the casing, although rippled in places, is at least reasonably clean for the period. Among the modifications undertaken to the original engines was the removal of a piece of casing between the front of the cylinders and the front framing; according to the late John Click, this was because when it was in place it restricted access to necessary lubrication for the front bogie. No 34057 had originally been earmarked for preservation by the Bulleid Society, but was destined to be withdrawn in May 1967 and subsequently passed over in favour of No 34023 *Blackmore Vale*.

Bottom: If cleaning was generally limited, it was non-existent for many of the BR Standard types, typified by the shocking external appearance of Class 4 No 80139 at Basingstoke on 21 January 1967 while probably undertaking pilot duties as well as shunting. It is perhaps just as well that there are no visible signs of ownership – who would want to admit to owning something in such a state? But beauty or otherwise is clearly only skin (or, more appropriately, 'dirt') deep, for the engine would remain in service until the end of steam.

And speaking of dirt … according to Jim's notes, 'No 34021 (formerly named *Dartmoor*) was believed to have been the dirtiest Pacific in the last 12 months!' – a statement no doubt open to dispute. (The Editor's take on this is that No 34077 would surely have been a contender as well, but then so might 350xx, 34xxx, etc, etc.) Whatever, No 34021 is seen here at Basingstoke with the 08.46 Bournemouth to Waterloo train on 21 January 1967. Alongside, the MAS colour light signals represent the new era, while the water column and sadly No 34021 are definitely the 'old' railway.

Above: Seen broadside as it departs, perhaps Jim was right after all – an extremely grimy No 34021 now passes underneath the gantry, its every move and turn under scrutiny. Did we really wear bobble hats at the time…?

…and getting away. For its final months, No 34021 was a Nine Elms engine and, while the depot staff were doing their level best to keep what engines were left running, cleaning was not a priority.

No 34037, formerly *Clovelly*, sports a pitted smokebox door while awaiting departure from Waterloo in late 1966 with the 'Bournemouth Belle'. On 10 August 1963 an unknown member of staff wrote to the Works Manager at Eastleigh suggesting that consideration should be given to the design of a 'suitably ribbed and flat smokebox door (for the Bulleid designs) … to obviate pressings'. This would seem to have come about as an audit of available stores revealed that there were only sufficient spares remaining to cover the next 12 months. Fortunately nothing came of this proposal and the remaining engines would see out their days with the original design. Certainly views exist of engines minus doors (No 34067 was depicted on the scrap road at Eastleigh without a smokebox door). With an ever-dwindling fleet, it would therefore appear that the available spares isere in the end deemed sufficient, likely supplemented by some cannibalisation and swapping in the final years.

No 34100 *Appledore* is as clean as No 34021 had been dirty. We should not forget that Bulleid engines were officially designated 'mixed traffic' and, while perhaps not totally the ideal motive power, it is very likely this was all that was available for this particular working. Jim only describes it as a 'light goods', seen near Earlsfield on 4 November 1966.

The Bournemouth electrification was intended to 'go live' at the start of 1967, but delays in the delivery of the new rolling stock meant that this date had to be put back to June, then eventually July 1967. As these delays became known, the decision was made to effect works repairs on a limited number of steam engines, the last of these being on No 34087 in 1966. Despite this, there was still a dwindling number of available steam locomotives, and in consequence new diagrams were brought into use on 2 January 1967, which effectively reduced the scheduled number of steam workings on the Bournemouth main line to about 19 daily. Already the prestige 'Bournemouth Belle' had been booked for diesel haulage on Sundays at least since 1 May 1966, but was now scheduled to be diesel-hauled on weekdays as well. From Waterloo steam departures were now at 08.35, 10.30, 11.30, 13.30, 15.30, 18.30 and 22.35. In the reverse direction steam was scheduled for the 06.22, 06.56 and 08.46 trains from Bournemouth, the 09.21 from Weymouth, then further Bournemouth departures at 09.24, 11.07, 13.25 and 15.50. Just two Salisbury-line trains were steam-worked, the 17.09 and 18.54 down and the 18.38 up. There was one additional Saturday service, the 12.30 to Basingstoke, rostered to be hauled by a BR Standard Class 4. In addition there were of course boat trains such as this one, with an unidentified Class 5 coupled to the usual mixed rake.

The first of the evening Salisbury commuter trains, the 17.09 Waterloo to Salisbury service, is seen between Waterloo and Vauxhall behind No 34071, formerly named *601 Squadron*. This engine was taken out of service in April 1967.

On 9 February 1967 there was a requirement for no fewer than three special trains in connection with the sailing of the *Oriana* from Southampton. Jim did not record the motive power for the first two workings, but for the third train Nine Elms turned out No 34104 *Bere Alston*, unusually still carrying its nameplate at this late stage. Complete also with headboard, the engine was recorded running light through Vauxhall en route to Waterloo.

Above: And now earning its keep, despite the obvious steam leaks from the various cylinder glands everything looks in fine fettle on what should be a non-stop run to Southampton Docks. Timings on these boat trains were generally fairly relaxed as they would be fitted into 'Q' paths, an available pathway for an extra service if required.

Right: Another boat train on 1 April 1967 sees No 73085 at the head of the 09.20 'Capetown Castle' working awaiting departure from Waterloo. We are not to know if a headboard was being carried although, if it was, it would likely have read 'Union Castle Line', whose vessels operated between Southampton and Cape Town.

Steam workings were curtailed even further from 3 April when the erstwhile 10.30, 11.30 and 13.30 services from Waterloo were re-diagrammed for diesel haulage. In the up direction, the 13.25 and 15.30 from Bournemouth were similarly affected. At the same time, the down Channel Island boat train, the 08.30 departure, was brought forward and now left at 08.10. Operationally, the end of April would also witness the fleet down to only about 75 active steam engines. This example is No 34019, formerly carrying the name *Bideford*.

Standard tank No 80016 departs from Southampton Central westwards on 6 April 1967.

Most of Jim's photographic forays were centred around the London area, although as we have seen he did venture to Basingstoke and Southampton. There were just two images further west, both at Lymington Junction, where he recorded Class 4 No 76008 on a three-coach local on the approach to Brockenhurst. At the rear of the train, the Lymington branch may be seen diverging to the left, while on the opposite side of the line is the trackbed of the former 'Castleman's Corkscrew' through Ringwood and Wimborne, which had closed to passengers in May 1964. The service is the 14.52 Bournemouth to Southampton Central – note also the conductor rails, which had also been energised by this time.

In the opposite direction Jim was able to view No 34024, formerly *Tamar Valley*, with the down 'Bournemouth Belle' service. The date is 6 April 1967, which goes to prove that even having been diagrammed for diesel haulage for the past three months. reliability and/or availability problems meant that a reversion to steam took place on a number of occasions.

The Mid-Kent Railway
Part 2

(Continued from Southern Way 35)
Jeremy Clarke

At a little more than 11 miles from Charing Cross, the line comes to Elmers End. This station opened with the line, the only intermediate stopping point at the time between New Beckenham and Addiscombe. How the location got its peculiar name is open to conjecture and theory. The more romantic – and mythical! – is that a well-known highwayman named Elmer met his End on a gibbet at the local crossroads, the other that many elm trees grew in the vicinity, hence 'Elms End'. The fact that the place was known as Elmers End for at least a decade before the railway arrived puts to bed the idea that the Mid-Kent beefed-up 'Elms End' to make it sound a little grander. Perhaps local vernacular pronunciation of Elms End was responsible, who knows? (Incidentally, the station name originally boasted an apostrophe, but this was later deleted.)

Whatever the case, the line is bridged at the London end by Elmers End Road, from which access to buildings and offices on both sides of the station was obtained, that on the up side being the main one as usual. The present building is not the original, which was lost with the major reconstruction of the station required by the opening of the branch to Hayes in 1882. That second building was reminiscent of the one at Clock House, but it did not survive the severe damage caused by a fire in December 1973. The present one, a tall steel-framed glass box, is best Network SouthEast 'brutal' and of doubtful architectural merit. The SECR footbridge, roofed in curved corrugated iron, still stands south of this building,

As a result of the opening of the Hayes branch, the platforms were raised and rebuilt with south-facing bays, both being accessible to incoming Hayes trains. The signal box then stood in the 'V' of the junction. A compact coal depot of three sidings was also established on the up side, accessible from the forecourt; it closed in May 1963. The down-side platform was seriously

This is the rear elevation of Elmers End signal box. A standard SECR structure from 1882, it contained a frame of 43 levers and was in use until 1975. *John Scrace*

Elmers End viewed looking north in 1954. The goods siding is on the left. Nine years after the cessation of hostilities, the station still shows evidence of wartime blackout painting. In 1961 a new platform canopy was provided on the down platform.

damaged during Second World War air raids, the canopy being left with a large gap until complete renewal in 1961. The bombers may have been aiming at the adjoining engineering works, which were also damaged, as were the nearby rows of terraced properties. That whole area was eventually cleared and is now occupied by a superstore and its car parks, and a bus stand. The tall brick building on the down side housing the rotary converters provided at electrification may also have been a target. It survives.

Platform extension, which affected all the stations on the line with the introduction of ten-car trains in 1957, was carried out at the south end. As a result the layout here was slewed to the extent that both the Hayes and Addiscombe lines passed to the east of the box with the junction now right in its shadow. Earlier track alterations had seen access from the Hayes line to the up bay abolished. Further platform extension for 'Networker' trains had to be done at the north end, which required complete reconstruction of the Elmers End Road bridge to provide a wider span.

The Chaffinch Brook now heads away south-eastwards to its source at the appropriately named Spring Park, while the Addiscombe line curves very gently more towards the south-west, climbing as it does so on a 1 in 120 gradient. South Norwood Country Park is on the up side for the first half-mile. Once the site of Croydon Corporation's sewerage works and refuse destructor, a private siding trailed from it into the up line; it did not survive beyond the 1940s.

Woodside station (12m 8ch) opened in 1871, principally to serve Croydon Racecourse. The brick building survives on the overbridge at the north end, a near-replica of that at Clock House. The station received the suffix '& South Norwood' in October 1908 and retained it for 46 years. Perhaps this represented a degree of retaliation against the Brighton's Norwood Junction, three-quarters of a mile away, which also had 'South Norwood and Woodside' appearing on its running-in boards for much of that time.

A coal yard consisting of a single siding had been squeezed into a small space behind the up platform in 1878, its connection trailing into the down line with a trailing single slip in the up one where it crossed. The yard closed at the end of September 1963. The signal box, some 70 yards beyond the down platform, came into service in 1877; it worked the junction when the Selsdon line opened, a down bay being provided for branch traffic. Following electrification, however, Elmers End became the terminus for branch shuttles, particularly as, over time, increasing demand on the Hayes line saw the bulk of 'through' London services working in that direction.

The down starting signals at Woodside were unusual, in Mid-Kent terms at least, in being mounted on tapering timber dolls supported by a perforated concrete post, a not unusual SECR arrangement. These were lost when the platforms were extended for ten-car working, new SR upper-quadrant signals being attached to LSWR-type lattice dolls on a post consisting of that Southern speciality, four worn running rails braced together. They had, perforce, been moved further south to stand right by the refurbished box, whose entrance steps now met the foot of the platform ramp. However, the two routes were still deemed to be of equal importance until the Selsdon line closed on 13 May 1983, after which the box continued in use for another 13 months. BR had first proposed closure of the Selsdon branch in March 1963, but opposition saw it reprieved for three years though it appears to have led a charmed life to carry on for much longer than that.

The Selsdon route diverged 12 chains beyond Woodside, the Addiscombe line now climbing at 1 in 300 for much of the way to the terminus 12¾ miles from Charing Cross. The name Addiscombe emanated from Adscomb House, which became Addiscombe Place following reconstruction in 1702 and its later use as a Military Seminary of the East India Company. At its opening as 'Addiscombe Road', the station had two platforms with the building part way along the up one, which had a bay behind it. Both platform lines led directly on to a turntable. There was no goods yard beyond a loading bank reached by a single siding trailing directly into the up line. The signal box was also on the up side at the station throat.

The station was comprehensively reconstructed in 1899 by which time it had been surrounded by housing. A handsome SER-style red-brick building faced directly on to Lower Addiscombe Road behind a small forecourt fronted by a pillared wall and iron railings. The up platform was widened and made into an island by extensions of the former bay road, which had a berthing siding laid alongside it. (That road was never electrified.) A new engine siding was provided north of the station on the up side, the turntable being transferred there. The connection to the up line from the single goods siding was moved further north, thus lengthening it. A larger signal box was provided in more or less the same position.

Further substantial change occurred at electrification, even the name: the station became 'Croydon (Addiscombe Road)' in April 1925. The turntable and engine road were removed, the resultant space being used to increase the goods yard to three long sidings, a 5-ton crane being set by the western one. The most noticeable change took the form of a four-road carriage shed on the down side. This was 510 feet long, each road thus accommodating eight coaches, and was used for cleaning and inspection only as well as being a 'signing-on' point. A new shed was built close to the former engine shed at Slade Green to carry out Eastern Section electric train maintenance and repair work. Electric services out of Charing Cross and Cannon Street were scheduled to begin on 1 December 1925, but delays in the power supply infrastructure caused it to be postponed for three months. The station name changed again then, the 'Road' suffix being deleted, and a final change saw it become plain Addiscombe in June 1955.

'Modern' electrification: 4-CEP No 7139 is seen soon after delivery. *British Railways*

Following extension for ten-car working in 1957, the ramps of the platforms embraced the signal box, causing the No 1 platform road to be moved to pass behind it. Platform 3, on the down side, was closed and removed at that time to permit an additional berthing siding to be put in. New rail-built signal posts graced the remaining two platform ends. The goods yard closed in 1968.

The demise of the station and, indeed, the whole of the line south of Elmers End was first mooted in 1990 in accordance with proposals for a tramway system in Croydon. This had gained support from London Transport and Croydon Council and followed a London-wide study of the City's transport problems carried out jointly by London Transport and British Rail in 1986. Following public consultation in 1991, during which the proposal was very favourably received, Royal Assent to the Croydon Tramlink Bill was given to London Regional Transport on 21 July 1994. Addiscombe closed after the last train on Saturday 31 May 1997. The signal box had been burned down the previous year, leaving the branch to be worked as a single line for the final few months of its existence. As the station itself was not included in the Tramlink scheme, demolition of all the buildings and clearance of the site did not occur until 2001, and it has since been completely redeveloped for residential occupation. The road into the development from Addiscombe Road is appropriately named East India Way.

While on the subject of Tramlink, it is convenient to return to Woodside and consider the Selsdon line. This curved away southwards from the junction, briefly rising at 1 in 70 then levelling out on an embankment before bridging both the main A222 Lower Addiscombe Road and Bingham Road to come to Bingham Road station (12m 67ch). This was in the heart of developing residential Addiscombe, which accounts for it being opened as a halt on 1 September 1906, sited south of the eponymous road. Wartime closure in March 1915 turned out to be rather more than temporary; the station did not reopen until electrification of the branch in September 1935, being upgraded then from its 'Halt' status. The upgrade included provision of new steel canopies and back walls to the platforms made of Exmouth Junction concrete. Entrances from Bingham Road led up to the platforms under covered staircases.

The line then began a steady rise as it approached the foot of the dip slope of the North Downs and passed through three short tunnels in close proximity to one another, Woodside (166 yards), Park Hill (122 yards) and Coombe Lane (157 yards). Within sight of the last came Coombe Road station (13m 68ch), which opened with the line but as Coombe Lane Halt. There were entrances on both sides, but the building was behind the up platform. A signal box was provided at the south end on the up side, though its use was increasingly rare. This was another wartime station closure, though it had been slated for this as early as 1894, but legal restraints prevented it. Electrification saw it reprieved again but as Coombe Road in line with the change of that road's suffix and upgrading as the A212. (The eastern end of Coombe Lane did not have its suffix changed and still exists as such.)

The line bridged Coombe Road and, heading approximately south-south-west, now ran gently downgrade to Selsdon, 14 miles and 31 chains from Charing Cross. In the course of this section it passed the site of Spencer Road Halt, about half a mile beyond Coombe Road. This was a simple wooden affair opened in 1906 with access from a public footpath crossing the line by way of a lattice girder bridge. Gates at the bottom of steps from the bridge opened on to the short, timber platforms. This was another wartime casualty, but the supposedly temporary closure proved to be permanent.

Selsdon, which had a 'Road' suffix to its name until the line from Woodside reopened, had platforms on both the Mid-Kent and Oxted lines, the junction between the two being 8 chains to the south. The main entrance was in the 'V' of the converging routes, reached by a steep access road from the north. But there was also access on the down side of the Mid-Kent from Selsdon Road itself, the B275. The Oxted-route platforms were spanned by a footbridge, but a subway ran between those of the Mid-Kent.

There was a substantial goods yard here consisting of five lengthy sidings and a dock road behind the Mid-Kent's down platform. Access was by trailing points at the up end of both the up and down lines. As early as 1894 storage facilities were established here by the Anglo-American Oil Company, and although the yard closed on 17 November 1968 these facilities continued in use and indeed survived the line's 1983 closure for all but ten years, to March 1993. In that period access was via a single lead off the Oxted line with the run-round loop much extended towards Coombe Road. Since closure the yard area has seen some industrial development.

The North signal box was by the yard points, although its responsibilities were assumed by the Junction box, at the south end of the Oxted line up platform, when the branch reopened. Not surprisingly perhaps, the two boxes differed, North being of SER design, South being typically Brighton. The signals on the Mid-Kent line at each end of the station showed similar differences.

The whole station had been closed in 1917, although the Oxted-line platforms were reopened on 1 March 1919. However, with South Croydon on the Brighton main line less than half a mile away, passenger demand for the service here was never heavy. After the Second World War traffic declined to three morning rush-hour London-bound trains, but none at all called in the evenings. The fact remains that Selsdon itself was some 1½ miles away and 300 feet higher than the station, making suppression of the 'Road' suffix unwarranted. Even before Beeching came on the scene, the decision was made to close the Oxted platforms; there was little protest before it happened, on 14 June 1959.

The Mid-Kent section, however, continued in use, all stations from Lewisham southwards having platforms extended to 540 feet in length where necessary to accommodate eight-coach electric trains. A similar lengthening was undertaken with the 1955 scheme to introduce ten-car trains on Eastern Division services in June 1956. Such expenditure could be justified by the heavy commuter traffic on the Hayes line, but by no stretch of the imagination were stations on the Addiscombe or Selsdon lines deserving of this, though they got it. A two-coach unit usually sufficed, even in the rush hour. Significantly Sanderstead station, where Selsdon-route trains terminated, was never extended beyond eight coach lengths until required to accommodate three three-car DEMU sets when diesel working over the Oxted line was introduced in June 1962. All remaining Mid-Kent stations can now accommodate 12 coaches of 'Networker' stock.

The whole of the former Mid-Kent route between Elmers End and the site of Coombe Road station now comes under Tramlink. Very considerable infrastructure changes were made for the trams, the most noticeable being the removal of embankments and demolition of some bridges at the southern end. The tram line now crosses both Lower Addiscombe Road and Bingham Road on the level, with the Addiscombe tram stop lying conveniently between them and some 600 metres east of the former Addiscombe station. And the Lloyd Park stop, just to the east of the site of Coombe Road station, has similarly been laid at ground level as a result of the removal of the embankment approaching the station. (The bridge abutments and matching embankment on the south side of Coombe Road are still there.)

The up bay platform at Elmers End remains as it was, the tram track being raised to bring the tram floors to that level. The Arena tram stop, at the south-west corner of the Country Park, is where the line from Beckenham Junction curves in. This runs along the south-west side of the Park and also uses 1¾ miles of trackbed of the former up line to Crystal Palace east of Birkbeck Junction. That route's down line is now bi-directional over that length.

Woodside station building still exists but is shuttered and out of use, while the platforms were demolished and platforms at tram height put down instead. Another stop, Blackhorse Lane, is sited very close to Woodside Junction, that road bridging the two former lines just to the south of the point of divergence. The trackbed towards Addiscombe is still clearly traceable beyond this point and, indeed, part of it is named Addiscombe Railway Park. The Blackhorse Lane stop is also very close to the source of the Norbury Brook, a tributary of the Wandle. It meanders northwards through Selhurst, flowing there in the open, north of the Rolling Stock Maintenance Depot, then on via Thornton Heath and Norbury to join the River Graveney before the confluence with the Wandle at Summerstown, north-west of Tooting.

From the Addiscombe stop, the tram line continues to use the Mid-Kent trackbed as far as Coombe Road. However, it is no longer direct because as soon as the track passes beneath the original bridge at Addiscombe Road (A232) a very sharp 90° curve points it westward to the Sandilands stop and on towards central Croydon. A similarly sharp 90° curve permits the New Addington line coming in from Coombe Road to make a junction at Sandilands, but the two sides of that 'triangle' are not joined by a third; thus there is no longer any 'through' working as there once was. (There is, incidentally, a Coombe Lane tram stop east of Lloyd Park.) Operation throughout the Tramlink system began in May 2000.

Having then disposed of modern developments, let us return to Elmers End and the one remaining Mid-Kent branch, to Hayes. This leaves Elmers End on a sharp, check-railed curve, the line turning through some 120° to head almost due east and climbing, mainly at 1 in 89, before reaching Eden Park (12m 34ch). Situated on an embankment with a subway beneath, the timber buildings on the up side, which also have access from a footpath from the south, were reconstructed in SER style prior to electrification, with new arc-roofed canopies on the platforms. There is no cover at all on the down platform now, and a Southern Railway canopy has replaced the arc-roofed one on the up side. The topography, not to mention the rural aspect, did not permit a goods yard here, nor was there much in the way of passenger business until electrification encouraged rapid and widespread housing development in the station's vicinity. The signal box, at the country end, did not see out the 19th century.

Now facing south-east, the line continues to climb, though on easier gradients, to West Wickham (13¼ miles). En route it crosses the Beck and passes the site of a trailing connection into the up line of a mile-long siding installed in 1929 to transport building materials for the Bethlem Royal Hospital at Monks Orchard, the western extremity of Beckenham. The site eventually had almost 2 miles of standard-gauge track within it as well as 3 miles of narrow-gauge 'temporary' track. The hospital opened in 1930, the siding being removed shortly afterwards, but its route is now marked by Monks Orchard Road, lined on the east side by terraced houses of the period.

Eden Park shopping parade and station entrance are seen in this postcard view of 1935, by which time the transformation of open country to suburb was almost complete, although the council's preferred renaming of the area as 'South Beckenham' was never put into effect. *Nancy Tonkin collection*

The up platform and buildings at Eden Park undergo some much-needed renovations in 1921 before the area was transformed. *H. J. Paterson-Rutherford*

This is West Wickham station in 1921 looking towards Eden Park, with the dock line for horseboxes behind the signal box just visible in the background. *H. J. Paterson-Rutherford*

The up-side buildings at West Wickham were wrecked after a bombing raid of 1 November 1940. *Southern Railway*

Some idea of the clientele expected to use West Wickham station may be gleaned from the provision of only one siding for goods traffic but two carriage loading docks, one on each side at the London end. The station buildings, on the up side with the SER-type of covered footbridge at the country end, were seriously damaged by bomb blast in 1940. A pleasant if unassuming building in brick was constructed after the war.

Electrification brought the usual rash of semi-detached but good-quality residential development, so much so that in the ten years following it ticket sales rose by more than 500% while season tickets issued went from 336 to 18,711, an astonishing rise of more than 5,500%. Not surprisingly, freight traffic increased too, particularly domestic coal, with an additional siding being laid in the down-side yard, which closed about 1963. A small signal box was located on the up side by the points of the siding into the loading dock.

The line is still climbing at about 1 in 400 as it heads for Hayes, but the immediate approach is downhill at 1 in 140. This section is in the form of a large-radius arc in which the line turns due east, although a sharply curved last few yards turns it back east-south-east as it enters the station at 14 miles and 34 chains from Charing Cross. Only one platform was provided here at first, the line from it, as at Addiscombe, leading to a turntable at the extremity of the platform. This saved a point by permitting direct access to the run-round loop. The up-side goods yard consisted originally of two sidings, one having a crane beside it and ending at a dock butting up to the forecourt. Another with a crossover to the first was added in 1899 when the dock road was effectively shortened by having the pointwork for a bay platform let into it. The goods yard closed in April 1965, although coal merchants continued to use it for rather longer and engineers took possession of the sidings until the beginning of 1971.

At electrification, the turntable was removed and the signal box shifted from the down side by the station throat to the opposite side of the track. (As it is fed from the rotary converter at Elmers End, the branch is equipped with an additional rail laid in the four-foot to assist return current flow.)

But the inevitable increase in traffic following this saw the station undergo a much wider transformation. As at West Wickham, rapid local housing development had seen a spectacular rise in ticket sales in the ten years from 1925.

The station building, which also incorporated the station master's house, was demolished to permit the bay to be extended across its site. A new building went in where the turntable had been. This was in the Southern's brick and rendered style of the period with shops within the structure facing both the concourse and the small forecourt. The goods sidings were lengthened at the same time. These works were completed by 1935. The building was damaged during the Battle of Britain and not completely repaired until 1956, and then not quite as the original design. It survives in that condition.

When the first phase of the Mid-Kent opened there were eleven down and ten up workings between London Bridge and Beckenham (Junction), all but three down and two up conveying 3rd Class passengers. Five each way sufficed for Sunday traffic, though there was at that time the usual 2-hour 'Church Interval' in the mornings. By 1869 nineteen trains ran each weekday to/from Addiscombe, of which eighteen gained/shed Beckenham Junction portions at New Beckenham, some of which continued on to or had emanated from Bickley, something of a surprise considering the animosity between the two antagonistic companies. There were six trains to/from Bickley on Sundays, of which four carried an Addiscombe portion.

This is Beckenham Junction looking towards Southend Road bridge, showing the narrow, steep stairs to the footbridge over which passengers had to hurry to change trains (on one occasion with a fatal result), and the well-stocked bookstall on the up platform. *Tony Harden collection*

Augmentation of the overall service followed the opening of the Hayes line, which was provided with nine down and eight up trains between Elmers End and Hayes. This had risen to thirteen each way by 1890, with four return trips on Sundays. From mid-August 1885 there were nine shuttles each way between Woodside and Selsdon Road but no Sunday trains. The working companies took it turns to run the branch, the annual changeover date for the working companies being

1 July. (The concept of a jointly owner/operated branch being worked on alternate years by different companies was not unique. The same applied between Fratton and East Southsea, this time involving the LBSCR and LSWR. In the latter case, and almost in comical fashion, each would literally pick up their respective paperwork each 31 December, with the new incumbent bringing his ready to start work the very next day.)

From 1906 all the Selsdon-line trains were worked by railmotors to permit the newly opened and unstaffed halts at Bingham Road and Spencer Road to be served. The guard was responsible for collecting fares and issuing tickets, not, one would have thought, a particularly onerous task. By 1914 Selsdon Road saw twenty-one trains each way. Railmotors continued to provide most of the service but some trains now worked through to Elmers End and even to Lewisham. However, there were still no Sunday workings and all weekday trains were withdrawn from 15 March 1915, though the line continued to function for freight and other 'through' traffic.

By that time the Hayes line, still very rural, saw eighteen trains each way – ten on Sundays – while for the first time Addiscombe had a more frequent service than Beckenham Junction, thirty-four each way against thirty-one. (This was to be the zenith for the latter's traffic.) Thirteen and fourteen trains respectively provided the Sunday service. Immediately before electrification the Addiscombe and Hayes lines had both seen frequency rise with thirty-eight and twenty-one return workings respectively, fifteen and twelve on Sundays. With Saturday half-days very much a common feature of working in the City, there were differences in the Saturday service compared with the rest of the week. But the Beckenham Junction service had declined, to eleven weekday trains only.

The years following electrification saw a steeply rising trend in frequency as demand grew with the 'sparks effect', the Beckenham Junction service remaining the exception. At first, however, the general level of service was formed of hourly departures from both Cannon Street and Charing Cross for Beckenham Junction and Addiscombe, with a connection at Elmers End for Hayes. But there were ten departures from London for the two Mid-Kent termini in the hour from 5.00pm. In line with the previous steam-worked service, Beckenham Junction saw four of these trains terminating, two each from Charing Cross and Cannon Street. Addiscombe was in receipt of five services, three from Cannon Street and two from Charing Cross, one of which provided a shuttle connection at Elmers End for the Hayes branch, which also had a single 'through' train, this from Cannon Street.

But by the mid-1930s there had been something of a revolution. The Hayes line now had no fewer than fifty-eight trains each way on weekdays and thirty-four on Sundays, matching the level on the Addiscombe route. The Southern's high hopes for the Selsdon line following re-opening and electrification in 1935 in providing a regular half-hourly service from Charing Cross were overly optimistic. Very limited usage showed this provision to be unsustainable. It had been reduced to an hourly Elmers End/Sanderstead Monday-Saturday shuttle even before the start of the Second World War. The problem

This 1968 view shows the mechanised hoppers and conveyor belts of the coal concentration depot at Beckenham Junction, which replaced the general goods yard in 1966. It remained in use until 1982, by which time coal was no longer the principal fuel for domestic use. This site was also destined to be the last remaining railway goods facility in the area. *John Minnis*

for the line was that access or transport to other local stations having a more frequent and/or faster service to the capital was straightforward from just about anywhere along its route. Selsdon, for example, was in shouting distance of South Croydon, a fairly frequent bus service from close to Coombe Road took only a few minutes to East Croydon, and Bingham Road was by some way less than half a mile from Addiscombe. One can understand why a service of sorts continued in wartime, but it is much easier to question why, in the circumstances, the Southern Region did not 'bite the bullet' as it did with that other local loss-making branch, to Crystal Palace High Level, and close it in the 1950s. And even more relevantly, why was good money thrown after bad when it came to completely unnecessary platform lengthening for ten-car working? There would, of course, have been objections to closure, just as there were with the later proposal. But with other conveniently reached stations around, they must surely have been satisfactorily answered. Anyway, enough of politics!

Following nationalisation the still growing use of the Hayes branch is reflected in the pattern of off-peak workings that saw the Addiscombe service reduced to a half-hourly shuttle connecting with two of the four-per-hour London/Hayes trains at Elmers End. Sanderstead shuttles were hourly, a frequency that persisted when the winter 1958 timetable reduced Hayes trains to three an hour and Addiscombe shuttles also to hourly, alternating with them in the up bay at Elmers End. The format only lasted a year, the Sanderstead shuttle being withdrawn in November 1959 except in peak hours, and the Addiscombe

shuttle increasing to thrice-hourly in connection with the Hayes trains at Elmers End.

But the winter 1958 peak service makes interesting reading. Following the 5.20pm service from Cannon Street to Sanderstead there were eighteen more Mid-Kent down departures in 2 hours, though overall only six left from that terminus. Of the nineteen, six used the Ladywell Loop, so avoiding Lewisham, and only four called at St Johns. Hayes received the bulk of workings, ten in total, of which two, the 5.49pm from Charing Cross and the 6.6pm from Cannon Street, ran fast from London Bridge to Catford Bridge. By contrast, Sanderstead received only three direct trains, one of which, the 5.41pm from Cannon Street, was fast from London Bridge to Ladywell. Two later shuttles for Sanderstead connected at Elmers End. Addiscombe similarly saw a mixed service with four trains from Charing Cross and one from Cannon Street, together with three shuttles from Elmers End. The one train so far unaccounted for, the 6.55pm from Cannon Street, was the only one that made use of the whole of the original route, terminating at Beckenham Junction at 7.20pm. After the 7.15pm from Charing Cross to Addiscombe, only Hayes received a 'through' service. Yet, oddly, it was Sanderstead that saw twice-hourly shuttles – at 20- and 40-minute intervals – the last leaving Elmers End at 10.6pm, while the Addiscombe shuttle was hourly until 10.26pm, then approximately half-hourly until 12.39am, this making a connection with an up Hayes train but no down one. Incidentally, the standard timings for the shuttles were 12 minutes to Sanderstead and 5 minutes to Addiscombe.

No 21C134 *Honiton* is on the down 'Golden Arrow' service at Beckenham Junction in 1947. Stephen Townroe recalled one day having to travel on this service and, before departure, observing the guard opening the steam heat cock on the end of the last vehicle to ensure that there was a clear route for the steam heat throughout the train. (He commented that this was indeed 'good practice'.) He later noted that before halfway the guard later informed him most of the passengers had already dozed off...

Rolling stock on the Mid-Kent has naturally seen changes both before and after electrification. Unlike previous electrification schemes, those of 1925 for the Western and Eastern Sections were provided with some new stock. Fifty-five three-coach 3-SUB units were built by the Metropolitan Carriage & Wagon Company at its Saltley works, twenty-nine of which, Nos 1496-1524, were allocated to the Eastern Section. Symptomatic perhaps of the additional demand in the eastern suburbs, each coach in these sets had one compartment more than those for the Waterloo services. All these units were equipped with 300hp motors, which gave them a better rate of acceleration than that of earlier units. Later they had an all-steel trailer added to become 4-SUBs and were renumbered 4301-25 (Western) and 4326-54 (Eastern). These sets were very long-lasting, not being withdrawn until 1959-61. Ten of them had their motor coaches subsequently modified as two-coach de-icing sets latterly renumbered into the Departmental list as 011-20.

These units provided the prototype for another 105 very similar sets built at Ashford and Brighton for this scheme. But these sets, numbered 1401-95 and 1525-34, were constructed from withdrawn SECR four- and six-wheel steam compartment stock on new standard SR underframes. As with the new-builds, these sets also were later augmented by all-steel trailers.

Prior to this augmentation, it was customary at peak time to run two of these sets with a two-car trailer set between them. It was not unknown for out-of-course running to put things so out of sync that a single 3-SUB set had to run round its trailer set before the return journey. It is likely that such a situation was exacerbated by wartime operating conditions, leading the Southern to reach the seemingly obvious conclusion, rather late perhaps, that putting an additional trailer coach into a three-car set would eliminate such problems, a course of action instituted from about 1941. Later that year the first Bulleid-designed 4-SUB unit appeared, numbered 4101. This consisted of two nine-compartment Motor 3rds, an eleven-compartment Trailer 3rd and a Trailer Composite with six 1st Class compartments placed centrally between four 3rd Class. Just before this entered service on the Eastern Division, 1st Class was abolished on all suburban lines, so the compo was never used as such. Another unit, No 4102, came into service in 1944, and Nos 4103-10 arrived in 1945. Alan Williams describes these as 'the epitome of Bulleid pack-'em-in design', for six-a-side seating was allied to compartments of such narrow dimensions that passengers sat with knees virtually interlocked. Standing room was more or less non-existent. These ten units soon acquired the nickname 'Queen of Sheba' – as we are told that 'She came with a Very Great Train'! I can find no record of these units working on the Mid-Kent, although knowing the convoluted diagrams that squeezed out as much mileage as possible in a working day it is not unlikely.

Complaints about the tight accommodation and complete lack of comfort, particularly when overcrowding forced passengers to stand, meant that in the next lot of ten, Nos 4111-20 of 1946, each carriage had one compartment less. Fewer seats, yes, but more comfortable all round if there were standees. These sets were the first all-steel suburban units with the upright and slightly bowed front end to the motor coaches that persisted right through to the EPB stock produced to both SR and BR outlines. Sets Nos 4121-36 soon followed, but other than in the trailer 'composite' compartments gave way to saloons of two-by-four bays in the motor coaches and three-four-three bays in the other trailer. These sets would most certainly have been seen on Mid-Kent workings. Several more batches appeared up until the beginning of 1951, latterly mounting new all-steel bodies on the frames of withdrawn 3-SUBs.

Later that year the first 4-EPB set appeared, No 5001, which was essentially the later SUB unit updated. It was equipped with electro-pneumatic brakes and control gear – hence 'EPB' – lightweight 250hp motors, buckeye couplings (the MCW sets of 1925 had originally been fitted with the unsuccessful MCB automatic couplings, later removed), roller-blind route panels, and suppression of the separate drivers' entry doors. Sets Nos

London Bridge: 'Schools' No 30929 *Malvern* is on a Dover train.

5002-15 followed in early 1952, and thirty-eight more came into service in 1953/54. In the best Southern tradition of never wasting anything valuable, salvaged underframes were used. The different control systems meant that these sets could not be used with any other stock, which thus saw their introduction on specified routes. The Eastern Section was an early recipient, though the first units were allocated to Waterloo-Guildford via Cobham services. A new series, beginning with No 5101, was turned out from 1953, the same in all respects to the earlier sets except that Central-type motor bogies were used in place of the Eastern variety. The early sets were ultimately running on these also. A total of 213 4-EPB units entered service up to

the end of 1957 – numbers were 5001-53 and 5101-260 – and eventually worked on all three Sections of the Southern Region.

In the meantime a total of seventy-eight 2-EPB sets built to the BR 'standard' carriage profile for the Eastern Section ten-car scheme had been turned out from Eastleigh. Saloon layout was used throughout, two-by-four bays in the motor coach and five-plus-four bays in the trailer. Numbered from 5701, they were put into service between 1954 and 1956. From 1957 Eastern Section suburban traffic was entirely in the hands of EPB stock, of both four and two cars. 2-EPB unit No 5766 was destroyed in the Lewisham disaster in December of that year, resulting in the construction of a replacement, No

5779, in 1958. Nowadays all suburban traffic operated by the present franchise holder, South Eastern, is worked by stock in the 'Networker' and 'Electrostar' series.

Privatisation has seen increased frequency on the Mid-Kent line once more, with four trains an hour off-peak. At the time of writing the half-hourly service from Charing Cross runs fast between London Bridge and Ladywell, making use of the Ladywell Loop and reaching Hayes after calls at all stations thereafter in 38 minutes. The two Cannon Street departures each hour call at all stations via Lewisham and also take 38 minutes, though they run only 13 minutes behind the Charing Cross departures from Ladywell onwards. The same pattern is reproduced in rush hours but with intervals varying between 9 and 13 minutes beyond Ladywell. The final Cannon Street departure is at 20.00, and thereafter the line receives a half-hourly service from Charing Cross. A similar pattern occurs on Saturdays except that there is no 'peak' swell, and Sundays see a half-hourly service based on Charing Cross with calls at all stations via Lewisham.

The up service is comparable, with a rush-hour departure from Hayes every 10 minutes between 07.13 and 08.33, alternate trains running to Charing Cross and Cannon Street via the usual routes. The off-peak and Saturday and Sunday patterns mirror those in the down direction. This level of service is a reflection of the generally rising trend on the line since the beginning of this century. Despite a slight downturn during the recession, present yearly traffic levels to/from the Hayes branch vary between about half a million journeys starting/finishing at Eden Park and something in the order of 1.15 million at Hayes.

Elmers End saw a sharp spike in passenger numbers following the opening of Tramlink, which, in the 2010/11 year, rose to more than half a million boarding and alighting users here. South Eastern's annual passenger traffic at the station exceeds a million. It may be symptomatic of the upward trend continuing that all stations on the route have platforms capable of accommodating twelve 'Networker' coaches, though at the moment ten is the maximum number in use. But with the economy growing, trains of that length may be necessary in the rush hours before long. But more importantly for its future, the line is well used at off-peak times.

Bibliography

History of the Southern Railway, C. F. Dendy Marshall, rev R. W. Kidner (Ian Allan Ltd, 1963)

Sir Herbert Walker's Southern Railway, C. F. Klapper (Ian Allan Ltd, 1973)

South Eastern & Chatham Railway, O. S. Nock (Ian Allan Ltd, 1961)

London Bridge to Addiscombe, inc The Hayes Branch, Vic Mitchell and Keith Smith (Middleton Press, 1993)

Croydon (Woodside) to East Grinstead, Vic Mitchell and Keith Smith (Middleton Press, 1995)

Southern Railway Handbook, B. K. Cooper (Ian Allan Ltd, 1983)

Railways of Beckenham, Andrew Hajducki (Ardgour Press. 2011)

Railways of the Southern Region, Geoffrey Body (Patrick Stephens Ltd, 1989)

Southern Electric, 1909-1979, G. T. Moody (5th ed, Ian Allan Ltd, 1979)

Southern Electric Album, Alan Williams (Ian Allan Ltd, 1977)

An Historical Survey of Southern Sheds, Chris Hawkins and George Reeve (Oxford Publishing Co, 1979)

Railway Track Diagrams, Southern & TfL, edited by Gerald Jacobs (TRACKmaps, 2008)

Article by the author in *Backtrack* magazine, September 2006

Inevitably a number of websites have been consulted, in the main to confirm or clarify historical information gathered from elsewhere. Though I am very familiar with the Mid-Kent Railway and its routes, past and present, Google maps are invaluable in illustrating stations and areas I have not been able to visit recently. However, those sites to do with Tramlink and South Eastern timetables provided source material relevant at the time of writing.

I am grateful to David Bodill and Carl Stephens for dating the opening of Sainsbury's Lower Sydenham superstore.

A Southern Railway (cryptic) Glossary

The 'Boxpok' complaint.

Alan Postlethwaite

Absolute block	Buffer stop set in concrete
Adams O2 tank	Very light ale from the Old Testament
Admiralty Pier	No 30850 *Lord Nelson*
Advanced starter	Pressing of confit duck with orange chutney and caramelised onion bread
Air smoothed casing	Brylcreme
Allhallows-on-Sea	Fog horns off Dover
Andover	Temporary transfer to BR Western Region
Angerstein Wharf	A weird type of locomotive exhaust devised in Germany
Atlantic Coast Express	All stations to Torrington
Balloon coach	Portly manager of Brighton & Hove Albion

Beattie well tank	Water supply to a telephone company
Beeching	Hovercraft service to the Isle of Wight (closed)
Belpaire firebox	Two women at Victoria station in charge of coal scuttles and ash pans
Beluncle Halt	Anagram of 'Lance the bull'
Big Four	MN, WC-BB, 7MT, 9F
Billington	Centralisation of accounts
Birdcage stock	Pigeon traffic
Blower	Call to stoke the furnace while at rest
Bogie	One over the eight at Royal St George, Sandwich

Bournemouth Belle	Lady in a brown and cream suit with straight sides and vestibuled ends	Cannon Street	Change here for Woolwich Arsenal
Boxpoks	Medical complication on the Surrey Hills	Canterbury & Whitstable line	Pilgrim's Progress
Bricklayers Arms	Retirement home for London & Greenwich navvies	Castleman's Corkscrew	A boozy supper somewhere in the New Forest
Brighton Atlantic	An ill-fated shipping line between Shoreham and New York	Catch point	Place to collect the single-line token
Britannia	Locomotive with a shield, spear, helmet, high running plate and a truncated life	Channel Packet	Stormy weather en route to France
		Cheap Day Return	Livestock to and from Canary Wharf
British Transport Commission	Officer on Leave ticket	Clear signal	Get as far away as possible
Buffet car	A match truck	Coaling stage	Amateur dramatics in East Kent
Bulleid	Disgruntled workforce at Eastleigh	Communication cord	Early Wi-Fi
Bunker trimming	A 10-minute wait at Salisbury	Conjugated motion	eo, is, it, imus, itis, eunt (Latin 'go')
		Country end	Broadstairs
Calstock Viaduct	Coaches with a primitive PA system	Coupling rod	Shunting pole
		Cross London freight	Disgruntled crew of a Class 'W'
		Crystal Palace Low Level	A destination for the plebs to enjoy a bit of razzmatazz

'The Brighton Belle' awaits departure from Victoria … really? *J. R. Fairman*

'The Devon Belle', Nine Elms, 26 October 1960. What is perhaps most remarkable is that this train had not run since 1954... (I took exactly the same pic at the time – and still have it! CF) *South Western Circle, J. Eyers collection*

Dartford Lupe	Sighting of wolves in the Cray valley
Dendy Marshall	Authoritative history of SR goods yards
Deptford Creek	Imminent collapse of a railway bridge
Double heading	Management of the SECR
Double slip	Twins evading the ticket inspector
Double yellow	A sending-off from the booking office
Draw bar	Any platform buffet on a chilly evening
Drummond Greyhound	A regular at Catford dog track
Dumpton Park	BR scrapyard near Eastbourne
Effingham Junction	A place disliked by railwaymen
Elephant & Castle	More big ideas from the LCDR
Eustace Missenden	A remote station on the Kent & East Sussex line, scrupulously tidy
Ewer Street	Sheep station for Borough Market

Exeter Banker	Andrew Barclay & Sons
Flat bottom	A condition suffered by long-distance commuters
Flushing service	Automatic ballast feed
Fogging machine	Provider of platform tickets
Football Special	Wimbledon or Portsmouth winning the FA Cup. (The latter did a few years ago...)
Footplatemen	Cobblers
Ganger	One of the Cray brothers

'Flat bottom'? Might it even be 'flat top' – a reference to the shape of the 'Q1' alongside?

Gate Stock	LBSCR trains on the East London line	Loose-coupled	The Midland Railway and the LSWR
Golden Arrow	Game show hosted by Bob Monkhouse	Lower Quadrant	The LCDR
Goods yard	Unit used for calculating freight tariffs	Ludgate Hill	The City branch of William Hill
Gradient post	A signalman at Sole Street	Lyme Regis	Yet another shade of Southern green
Grain	Change here for Margate Sands		
Gravesend West	Overspill from Brookwood Necropolis	Maid of Kent	Vera Lynn singing 'There'll be Bluebirds over the White Cliffs of Dover'
Grouping	Six-a-side plus eight standees with umbrellas in a steamy 4-SUB compartment	Man of Kent	A hardy commuter from Ashford
		Marsh	The Hundred of Hoo branch
		Maunsell ducket	Warning on a 'Schools' Class to watch one's head
Hastings and Ore	Choice of stations at St Leonards	Metropolitan Extension	Carnage in suburbia
Havant	Lost luggage office	Mid-Kent line	Aspirations to live in the countryside
Hawkhurst branch	Careful avoidance of villages		
Headcodes	Bowler, homburg, trilby, beret and flat cap	Miniature lever frame	Hornby control panel
		Mixed traffic	Chaos at Clapham Junction
Holborn Viaduct	Old tobacco smoked in a long pipe	Multiple unit	More than one passenger on the Petrockstowe line
Hoo Junction Yard	A good place to park one's Tardis		
Hop Pickers' Special	Home brew	Night Ferry	Sir Edward Watkin's cab home
Horse box	London Bridge signalmen shouting from one end to the other	Nine Elms	Change here for Sevenoaks, Ash, Carshalton Beeches, Forest Row and Paddock Wood
Horsted Keynes	Anagram of 'The SER donkeys'		
Hump	Disgruntled staff at Feltham	North Kent East	A mythical location nowhere in Kent
		North Kent West	Anyone's guess – Erith, perhaps?
Improved Engine Green	Mustard, custard or bustard	No Smoking	Electrification programme
Injector	State subsidy		
Interlocking frame	The double-deck commuter train		
Ironclad	Rusty sheets with a positive charge		
Island platform	The down bay at Havant		
Leader	A locomotive that leads one up the garden path		
Light Pacific	A friendly electrician		
Liver & Bacon	Lunch on the Brighton Belle		
Locomotive Exchanges	A 10-minute wait at Exeter		
Longhedge Works	Experimental field boundaries on the Battersea marshes		

Nine Elms (Goods) – and not a tree in sight. *South Western Circle, J. Eyers collection*

The midday 'fruit express' at Paddock Wood. *W. A. Corkill*

Ocean Quay	Rudimentary access to Plymouth Sound
Ocean Terminal	The very last Cunarder
Odeon style	Queuing for a ticket
Off-peak	No 34095 *Brentor*
Old Kent Road	Redhill to Tonbridge for £60
One-paws-four	Caterham train at Purrley
Orient Express	Strong Java coffee
Outer Circle	Broad Street to Brighton via Willesden and Eridge; Whiskers on kittens etc...
Overhead electric	Utility bill for Waterloo station
Padstow	Removable headrests on the LSWR
Pagoda roof	Early Wainwright design for the bullet train
Passenger mile	Walking en masse from London Bridge station to the City
Passing loop	Bridge convention on a Brighton commuter train
PD&SWJR	Random letters typed by a monkey
Peckham Rye shed	Poultry farm near the Nelson Mandela Estate
Permissive block	Be it on your head if you proceed
Pick-up goods	Yard crane
Pilot	Auction of British Railways pork pies
Pines Express	Lament for the days of steam
Platelayer	A steward in the restaurant car
Plymouth Friary	The local chippie

Polegate	Change here for the Northern Line
Pony truck	Freight to Tattenham Corner
Portsmouth & Southsea	A shipping line to Tasmania
Portsmouth Direct	This way to HMS *Victory*
Port Victoria	Battersea Wharf
Power frame	Tessie O'Shea
Pullman	Manual shunting
Push and Pull	Boarding a District Line train at Victoria
Queenborough Pier	The Duke of Westminster
Queens Road	A superhighway between Battersea and Peckham
Radial tank	Hot water supply in the buffet car
Railway Executive	Any 1st Class passenger
Reading South	W. H. Smith on the down platform
River Class	Aquaculture course at Wye College
Rover ticket	Dogs only
Royal Wessex	Any locomotive of the 'King Arthur' Class
Running buffet	Fried egg sandwich with ketchup
Running shed	Seasonal flooding at Dover MPD
Run-round loop	The South London line
St Pauls	Renaming of Saul Street after a blinding flash
Saloon	A boozy coach
Sand drag	Rip tide at Bude

Saxby & Farmer	Potato traffic along the South Coast	Staggered platforms	Changing trains at London Bridge while carrying heavy luggage
Season ticket	Available on summer Saturdays	Starter signal	Semaphore arm that comes down with a thump
Sevenoaks cut-off	Hairdressing salon on the SER	Stewarts Lane	A classic Western starring James Stewart and Frankie Laine
Shortlands	Grain, Sheppey and Portland Bill		
Siding	Voting with the LSWR to do away with the Overhead Electric	Stroudley	A way of walking in the Brighton offices
Single-line working	A maiden hanging out washing	Sunny South Express	The PLM to Marseilles
		Surrey Docks	An apology for colliding with someone
Sir Brian Robertson	No 30782 photographed by an editor. (Definitely *not* guilty.)	Surrey Iron Tramway	Guided sight screens at the Oval
Slip working	Icy conditions on the North Downs	Sykes Lock & Block	A cunning plan in American football
Snow Hill	Evercreech Junction to Burnham-on-Sea	Szlumper	A type of semi-reclining sleeping car
Somerset & Dorset line	Autumn leaves near Weymouth		
Sorting sidings	Preparation of fish & chips	Ten compartment third	A bronze medal for sardines
Spa Road	Change here for Tunbridge Wells	Terrier tank	Water supply for the station master's dog
Spectacles	Nickname for Sir Herbert Walker	Theatre-type indicator	Directions to the last train home from Charing Cross
Staats Forbes	Anagram of 'Fast SER boats'	Thermic syphon	Bulleid techno-speak to bamboozle directors and enthusiasts
		Third rail	BR
		Three Bridges	Alexandra, Grosvenor, Hungerford
		Three-way point	Loughborough Junction
		Track circuitry	Meandering of 'The Man of Kent'
		Tractive effort	Sprinting to catch one's train
		Troop train	BP Special to Brownsea Island
		Turntable	Shift rota for the engine crew

Sherbourne wagon turntable, 21 March 1964. Was there a shift rota for wagons as well? *South Western Circle, J. Eyers collection*

<Image 80>

Upper Quadrant	The LSWR
Urie Arthur	A distant cousin of Yuri Gagarin
Vacuum brake	Dropping one's Thermos
Wagons Lits	Stock manufactured at Lee-on-Solent

Walchaerts valve gear	Poster about protective clothing	Withered Arm	Soldiers arriving back from Dunkirk
Watercress Line	Temporary closure due to flooding	Woking	Richard the 3rd Class passenger
West End of London & Crystal Palace Railway		Woolwich Arsenal	'No football 'ere, mate!'
	Beckenham Junction or bust	Workmen's train	The SR signalling school
Westinghouse	Concentration of signalling in the west	Wrong line working	Kent Coast Electrification
		Wroxall	Meldon traffic
West of England main line	Dublin to Belfast		
Wheel tapping	An Iron Age good luck ritual to keep passengers happy	X14 Class	Locomotives never seen by young spotters
Widened Lines	Early days on the Great Western		
Windsor lines	Facial ageing of the Royal Family	Z Class	Nodding off in a crowded commuter train

'Z' No 952 shunting at Eastleigh. By the look of it, far too much to do instead of nodding off.

Book Review

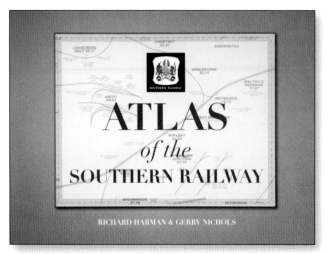

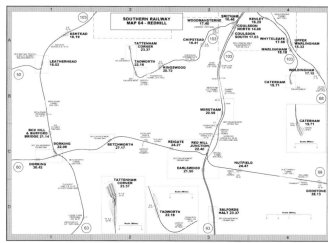

Atlas of the Southern Railway by Richard Harman and Gerry Nichols (Ian Allan Ltd, ISBN 978 07110 38295). 224pp, £30.00

We do not accede to many book reviews in 'SW', a deliberate policy, the intention instead being to concentrate on fact. Indeed, there has only ever been one before, for the recent HMRS 'LSWR' livery register, though it is now certainly time for the second.

Released by Ian Allan in May 2016 is *Atlas of the Southern Railway* by Richard Harman and Gerry Nichols. Readers of 'SW' will of course already know the extent of the Southern system: east to west, Folkestone to Padstow, and north to south, Reading to Ventnor – with of course numerous places in between. I suspect also all of us will be familiar with our own home 'turf', this area of knowledge expanding as we find interest in other areas perhaps in consequence of personal study, through reading other works (we hope in 'SW', of course!) or maybe even through research into a possible modelling prototype. But I would defy anyone to have a finger-tip knowledge of the system at every location – until now.

I will admit that when I first heard of the suggestion for this book I was of course elated that at last something covering the whole Southern Railway network was in the offing, but that was also tempered with one question. Would the new book actually give me what I personally – and I suspect others – would also want: accurate detail? And by detail I mean track layouts down to siding level and the changes associated with these. I need not have worried, as the result is something far more than I could ever have expected: the first comprehensive atlas of the SR replete with more detail than I could have expected. For those among us who take pleasure in studying old maps, this is the book for you. It is also for those interested in track layouts, the position of junctions and, if you are feeling particularly brave, studying the complexity of the lines around London – questions on this topic later... (no, not really).

If there is a fault it is not with the Atlas but with your reviewer – how best to represent the content with the single page example shown here? Whatever, we have chosen one at random, 'Map 64 – Redhill', but to be fair any of the 118 actual maps would have equally sufficed. (Note: the necessity to provide repeat maps where layouts changed, plus location enlargements, mean that there are far more than just 118 pages devoted to the maps.) It is also immediately clear that the authors have thought long and hard on how best to present their work, which starts with a series of illustrative map 'Keys', thus allowing quick and easy access to the location of interest. Where a location has changed significantly between 1923 and 1947 there is more than one map for the same location, and where necessary numerous individual stations, yards and junctions are also shown in enlarged form.

The temptation with any book of this type is of course to immediately turn to the area of one's own specific knowledge and, subconsciously perhaps, look for anything amiss. I personally found nothing, at the same time learning things I did not know.

The whole is supported by a series of indexes. Initially this takes the form of a comprehensive index, which is then subdivided into specific topics such as Bridges and Viaducts, EMU Depots/Engine Sheds and Works, Industrial and Military systems, Level crossings, Locations and Signal boxes, Sidings, Stations, and finally Tunnels.

Produced as a hardback to A4 landscape format, meaning that the book can be opened flat without the need to turn it through 90°, it is immediately seen as a quality production; there is even a bookmark printed with the symbols used on the various pages as a useful aide-memoir.

This is a work that should find a home on the shelves of every Southern enthusiast and a few beyond. Criticism? Yes, one. Simply that I wish I had had the opportunity to publish it myself!

A Brief Encounter at Midhurst Tunnel

The horseshoe shape of Midhurst Tunnel is clearly evident in this view of the eastern portal in 1964. *J. Grayer*

Jeffery Grayer

recalls the day that Midhurst Tunnel had its moment of fame in front of British movie cameras.

When recalling British movies that have used railway stations and other infrastructure as a backdrop, one immediately thinks of *Brief Encounter* at Carnforth, *Oh Mr Porter* at Cliddesden on the Basingstoke & Alton line, maybe *Rotten to the Core* with Anton Rodgers at both Christ's Hospital and Baynards on the Horsham-Guildford route, the latter also being used in a number of films including *The Grass is Greener* with Cary Grant and Deborah Kerr, *The Black Sheep of Whitehall* with Will Hay and *Die, Monster Die* with Boris Karloff, or perhaps Midford and Monkton Combe in *The Titfield Thunderbolt*. Less well known is the Boulting Brothers' comedy *Carlton-Browne of the F.O.* ('F.O.' being the Foreign Office), starring Peter Sellers and Terry-Thomas, part of which was filmed in 1958 at Midhurst's ex-LBSCR station and tunnel.

Above left: Carlton-Browne of the F.O. **is regularly aired on television and a DVD can also be obtained, although it is easy to miss the railway element for, as is often the way after hours of filming on location, it only occupies just a few seconds of the finished film.**
(https://en.wikipedia.org/wiki/Carlton-Browne_of_the_F.O.)

Midhurst closed to passengers when the Petersfield-Pulborough branch was shut on 7 February 1955, and since that time played host to goods services from Pulborough, the line onwards to Petersfield being closed entirely. Thus the location was ideal for filming purposes, with few other rail movements to interrupt progress. It also had the added bonus of an adjacent tunnel, which was vital to the plot of the film, and the station retained an impressive building in spite of years of neglect since passenger closure.

Although No 32640 was conveniently based nearby at Fratton depot in 1958, for use on the Hayling Island branch, it came up from Brighton for the day with a local Inspector. A spare coach was found and the entourage made their way to Midhurst via Pulborough and Hardham Junction on 17 July 1958. No 32640, dating from 1878, received embellishments such as a wooden cowcatcher and a balloon casing around the chimney, which were added to give the locomotive a 'Ruritanian'* look. The BR

* 'Ruritania' was a fictional country in Central Europe that formed the setting for three books by Anthony Hope, most notably *The Prisoner of Zenda*. The term is used today to indicate a hypothetical country, often with overtones of tinpot pomp and circumstance.

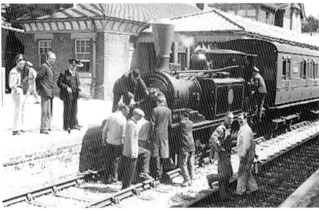

Peter Hay recalls the actual filming day: 'On the appointed day I drove over from Brighton and met Gordon Allaston, my area inspector, and Locomotive Inspector McCarthy. The film crew turned up in legions! I presume someone sent the film company a bill. It certainly made a change from holding enquiries into derailments and having to pump truth out of a well of assorted lies.'

crest on the side tanks was obscured, although the smokebox numberplate, 70F shedcode and cabside number were left in situ. The appearance of a 'Terrier' at Midhurst was not unprecedented, for in LBSCR days locomotives of this class were at one time allocated to Midhurst shed; from the 1880s until replaced by 'D1' tanks, 'Terriers' Nos 42 *Tulsehill* and No 77 *Wonersh* were familiar motive power at Midhurst.

Oddly enough, only a month before filming, on 8 June, a ramblers' excursion from Charing Cross to Midhurst proved to be the first passenger train to traverse the branch since closure three years earlier. Stovepipe chimney 'Q' Class No 30549 with eight well-filled coaches hauled the train throughout the day, taking the empty stock back to Horsham for cleaning before returning later in the day to collect the ramblers.

The day of filming fortunately proved to be bright and sunny, so did not necessitate a return visit either by the film crew or the locomotive. Briefly the story of the film concerns the partition of the fictitious island of Gallardia between two factions, this being taken to absurd lengths and visibly demonstrated by a man propelling a cricket-pitch white-line-marking machine through cottages, over a cow and into a railway tunnel (Midhurst), among other places. There followed a sequence when the whistle of a locomotive announced it was entering the tunnel, emerging from the other end of the tunnel complete with a white line up the front of the smokebox. The 'Terrier' was filmed minus its white partitioning stripe apparently going into the tunnel, although it was actually filmed coming out of the tunnel and the film reversed. The white stripe was then painted on and the engine filmed coming out in 'partitioned' condition. The fate of the partitioner and his machine in the face of an oncoming locomotive was not elaborated upon in the storyline!

Although withdrawn from BR service on 21 September 1963, shortly before closure of the Hayling branch, the locomotive 'star' of the film, No 32640, went on to preservation, initially as a static exhibit at Butlins Holiday Camp at Pwllheli, and latterly on the Isle of Wight Steam Railway, to whom it was loaned in 1973, then eventually sold for £3,500 in 1976. Having received a new boiler in 2010, it can still be seen in operational condition on the island today in its guise as No W11 *Newport*.

The other stars of the film were not so fortunate. Terry-Thomas died in 1990 after a long battle with Parkinson's disease, and Peter Sellers prematurely of a heart attack in 1980 at the age of just 54. Midhurst finally closed to goods traffic in October 1964 and the station was subsequently demolished in 1968 and housing built upon the site. The western portal of the 276-yard-long tunnel was boarded up and flats now occupy the site immediately in front of the entrance, while the eastern end is open, protected only by a length of metal railings. Following closure, responsibility for the tunnel was vested in British Railways Board (Residuary), although as this body was abolished in September 2013 it is now inspected by The Highways Agency Historical Railways Estate.

With grateful thanks to John Trueman, Editor, Midhurst pages, for permission to quote/copy from his website: www.violetdesigns.co.uk/midhurst_film_sets_carlton_Brown e.htm

The Lost Archives of Stephen Townroe

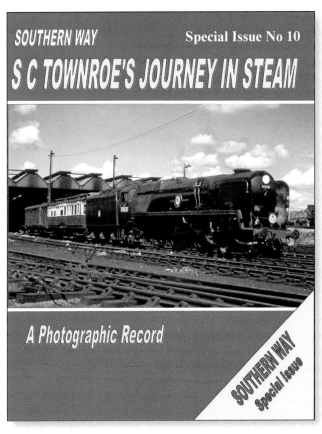

Regular readers of 'SW' and the various 'Special' issues will already be aware of 'Special Issue No 10' dealing with the railway career of Stephen Collingwood Townroe.

Having been privileged to see some of Mr Townroe's colour slides many years before, I had long wanted to undertake a book project, but this only became possible when three specific circumstances came together.

The first was agreement from Paul Chancellor at Colour-Rail to allow a viewing of the original material; those slides selected would then be scanned by Paul and placed on a disc. Next was Rod Blencowe's consent for a copy of the list of black & white images he had obtained direct from Mr Townroe several years earlier. Finally, and crucial to the project, was direct contact with the Townroe family, without whose enthusiastic support nothing could have been completed.

The finished book was released in April 2014 (up to June 2016 it had attracted seven Amazon reviews, all ★★★★★). So where is this leading? Well, certainly not a deliberate plug, but I do hope that, after what follows, those who may not have picked it up may be tempted to do so.

I had always had my suspicions that there was more material, particularly b&w, than was available from Rod Blencowe. That is certainly not in any way intended to infer criticism – more likely that Rod could criticise me for in the past having badgered him about what material he had, hence the importance of obtaining his list, showing everything he had available.

The reason I was still suspicious was that, when viewing some of S. C. Townroe's own railway writing, an Amazon list of his railway books was found at https://www.amazon.com/s/ref=la_B001KE4G0U_ B001KE4G0U _sr?rh=i%3Abooks&field-author=S.+C.+Townroe &sort=relevance&ie=UTF8&qid=1466421205. It appeared that

The earliest view in the collection, recorded as 'Eastleigh Loco Works: men working on injector, H15 class'. Being pedantic this would more accurately be 'fitter and mate/apprentice'. We have no date other than it comes from Album 1 'March 1937 though to October 1938' and, as the first image, it may be taken to be from the start of that period. The engine number was not given, although it could well be No 332, as the same negative strip contains two views of this engine. These were taken from the pit looking upwards and showing the front and the loco number; much else is missing and neither is really suitable for publication.

there were occasions when photographs had been reproduced that were certainly not in the Blencowe listing. I had put this down to the obvious, that material had been mislaid over the years, and there matters rested until June 2016, when out of the blue I received a telephone call from one of 'SCT's' daughters.

She had been searching through a box from 'Pop', which had reposed in the garage for several years ostensibly containing jigsaws. However, underneath was a different collection: fourteen books of b&w negatives, approximately one for each twelve-month period from March 1937 through to about 1953, including the war years. Each book contained (or to be more accurate had originally contained) an average of 108 strips of four 35mm negatives; if you want the maths, that is 432 negatives per album, so fourteen albums equals 6,048 individual views. After 1953 SCT had concentrated on colour slides.

However, the large number quoted should be seen only as a starting point, as one album was devoted solely to his marriage, while a high proportion from the remainder are similarly personal: family, friends, holidays, plus general non-railway scenes. It was also quickly apparent that it was from these albums that the b&w negatives now in the care of Rod Blencowe had come, but even so there was still a large proportion of unseen railway views – 837 to be precise – and I am grateful to the family for allowing me to borrow the original material to scan and use in 'SW' as appropriate.

There was a further bonus in that the albums contain the original annotation of the negatives, from which much useful information can be gleaned. This also provides detail and explanation relative to some of the b&w material previously used in 'Special 10'. I should also explain that this does not mean that we now have at our disposal 837 new and unseen images. More accurately, 'SCT', like all of us, had his failures – a poor day, poor composition, faulty film, camera shake, etc – which all combine to reduce the figure quoted. But fear not – this is not a statistical exercise and I am not addicted to counting. Finally, we have to allow that he would sometimes take a number of views of the same occasion whether of an accident or whatever. His index is often the only clue to what is occurring and, while dates are not always exactly given, in a worst-case scenario they can at least be assessed to within a twelve-month period.

The collection had not suffered any deterioration, despite its time in the garage. In addition, I was loaned three cassette tapes of railway sounds and some limited interview material. However, it is still the images that are by far the best. So, where to start? The obvious thing had to be at the beginning, but in this first article I have taken the opportunity to update the information from some of the views also previously published in 'SW Special 10'.

Soon after the earlier image come three views of the ill-fated Eastleigh railway museum housed in Paint Shop. It was here that the Southern Railway found a temporary home for the former Beyer Peacock 2-4-0T *Ryde* together with Mr Drummond's *Bug*, although neither appears to have been photographed by 'SCT'. (Does that mean that they had already moved elsewhere?) The location of the museum within the works implies that it was hardly open to the public either. What is interesting, though, are some of the exhibits shown, including a third nameplate from *Lord Nelson* (the other two would have been carried on the engine) and the three nameplates from the former Lynton & Barnstaple engines.

Left: This view was taken some months after the earlier image, but also clearly shows how artefacts were continuing to accumulate, including what is now a full set of nameplates from the former L&B engines.

Below: Other items in the museum included various hand-lamps, a coat of arms once used to decorate an LBSCR Royal Train engine, and a paint board.

'SCT' records this particular vehicle as a 'Saloon used by Queen Victoria', although the late Gordon Weddell is more accurate; this was in fact former LSWR Inspection Saloon No 9 dating from c1877. In Southern Railway days it had acquired the designation 073S and survived until at least 1939. 'SCT' recorded it at Eastleigh some time in 1938. It would be nice to think it was being considered as an addition to the museum but, like *Ryde* and the *Bug*, it would not survive and was instead broken up some time after 1939.

This particular view would do well as a quiz question; simply put, what is unusual about the photograph? The answer is in the Royal cipher – look carefully and it shows 'VIII' for Edward VIII, who was King just from January to December 1936. As none of the views is prior to March 1937, it is possible that this vehicle had arrived at Eastleigh for repainting.

The collection includes eight views, of which this is an example, of water troughs at Langley (LNER), taken on what appears to have been an official visit. While most of the party appear content to observe from the lineside, Stephen Townroe was more adventurous and climbed to the top of the actual tank to record the scene. Was this a visit prior to the consideration of installing troughs on the Southern? This would certainly appear the most likely explanation and, while the idea was obviously shelved during the war, it would come up again for discussion in 1948. (See article in 'SW6'.) Officially the role of 'SCT' on the Southern at this time was 'Technical Assistant to the Locomotive Running Superintendent'. This was a post he had commenced in September 1937 and would hold until he took charge of his first depot, Dorchester, in November 1938. Between the dates mentioned his job was the maintenance of locomotives in service, hence his attendance at the incident in the next set of images and similarly no doubt the fact-finding trip to Langley.

Most will be aware that, as a motive power officer, 'SCT' took a keen interest in derailments, such as here at Marden (Kent), where 'L1' No 1758 has suffered a failure of the rearmost tender axle, the actual break having occurred at the 'wheel-seat'. It is likely that this incident occurred some time in the spring or summer of 1938.

Corrigendum to caption information, 'Southern Way Special No 10: S. C. Townroe's Journey in Steam'

P25: Add 'This was the first engine to traverse the new line at Fawley.'

P61: It is confirmed that he transferred to Yeovil in April 1939.

P64, top: The 'WD' loco was newly delivered to Bricklayers Arms.

P64, lower: Other un-located images of No 901 on this occasion refer to 'Taking temperatures on Schools class loco'. We are not informed as to what test was being undertaken.

P91: The illustrations of the Whitaker tablet exchange apparatus came about as a result of an incident where the grab handle of the Great Western coach was struck and damaged by the tablet catcher. We are not told where, but it may well have been at Midford, as this is where the illustrations were taken. For the purpose of the tests, a paper tablet was placed in the holder and various runs made to check clearance, etc; the peg seen being used showed a 4½-inch clearance. We are not told if this was the correct clearance. 'SCT' was present for the tests, together with a Mr Ellcott. The conclusions were not stated but there were two possibly scenarios. The first and least likely was that the damaged vehicle was officially prohibited from the S&D, as it was simply too wide for the line. More likely was that the track itself had been subject to 'creep', resulting in the exchange apparatus being closer to the running line than was permitted. (Further views of this incident will be included in a later 'Lost Archives' article in 'SW'.)

P94/95: This was a trip 'SCT' made on No 21C110 from Guildford to Redhill. He recorded the name of driver Hunneywell.

P96, lower: The man in the bowler hat is now identified as Mr R. D. Steele, District Motive Power Superintendent, Nine Elms. The location is not given but it was recorded that the train was the 'Royal Wessex'. (An article on the life and career of Roy Steele appeared in 'SW27'.)

Further articles on 'The Lost Archive of Stephen Townroe' will appear in later issues.

Terry Cole's Rolling Stock Files
No 35 Some Ex-LSWR Coaches

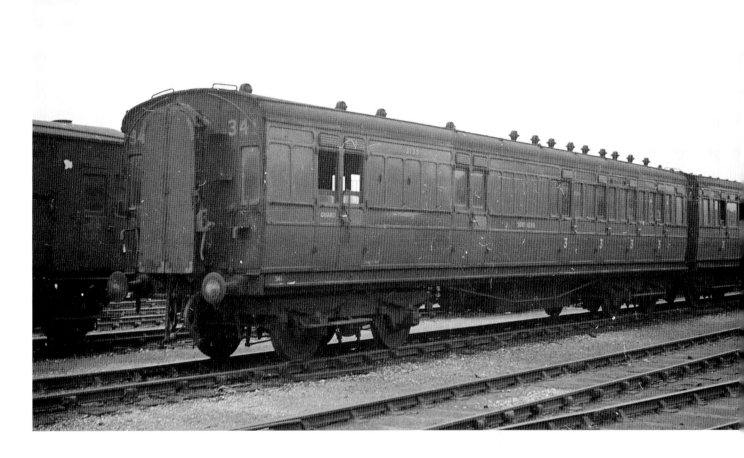

From the early years of the 20th century the London & South Western Railway introduced new corridor vehicles with inter-coach gangways for the Waterloo-West of England services. These designs, with slight variations in length, continued to be built until the final years of the LSWR when the 'Ironclad' designs superseded them. Significant withdrawals took place in the 1940s, although some survived into the 1950s, the last vehicles in traffic being withdrawn in 1957.

Here is 56-foot four-compartment Brake 3rd No 3133, one of the first to be built, having been constructed in April 1904. It has its corridor on the left-hand side (looking along the coach from the guard's compartment) and was (probably) built without side lookouts. These coaches were built in left-hand and right-hand versions with and without lookouts. Given the number 731 when new, it was renumbered 1856 before becoming SR No 3133 and being allocated the SR Diagram 131. It is seen here in Southern Malachite Green livery in set 341. One of the last survivors of its type, it was withdrawn in February 1957. *All photos taken at Eastleigh by Dennis Callender*

This is another early vehicle again in Southern Malachite and seen in set 341. It is a 54-foot Composite built in May 1904, and first given the number 5, then 2255. The Southern renumbered it again as 3075 to Diagram 277, and it was also withdrawn in February 1957. Part of a third vehicle of set 341, left-hand Brake No 3137, can be seen on the right.

This 57-foot eight-compartment 3rd is from one of the later batches and was built in December 1920. Allocated the number 143 by the LSWR, the Southern renumbered it 703 and Diagram 22. It is seen here in the very attractive Southern Malachite Green livery. It was withdrawn in November 1955 from set 338. Fortunately, LSWR 3rd No 494 (SR 673), built in 1911, survives at the Bluebell Railway awaiting restoration.

Rebuilt
The Letters and Comments Pages

We start with a piece from Alan Moon (and he is absolutely right, of course):

'I am sorry to say I disagree with your thoughts on the identity of the ex-LBSC 'Terrier' on page 45 (SW33). Yes, it is in Mr Stroudley's 'improved engine green' after restoration and yes, it is in front of Eastleigh Works, but I beg to differ over the

Above: **This image was located just after 'SW35' went to print and refers to 'Charles Anderson, Part 4', page 20. 'The survivor at Mottisfont (Hants). The up distant signal clearly shows its origins as a slotted post. Of course, this begs the question whether this the original signal post dating from 1865 or had it been recovered from elsewhere and reused? Note as this was a double line, it was a worked and not a fixed signal arm. This actual signal remained in use until the line closed in 1964.'** *Dr J. L. Farmer*

Right: **Another view that arrived too late for 'SW35' is this view of No 43260, which fell into the drain between Ascott and Shapwick on 26 August 1949 (see 'SW35', page 8). The engine was cut up on site.** *LGRP*

identity. You will know that the class is of particular interest, and of the class *Fenchurch* is my favourite. But this example is, I am reasonably sure, not *Boxhill*. The engine in the picture is an 'A1X' with an Isle of Wight-type extended bunker, eliminating the rear tool box.

'*Boxhill*, LBSCR No 82, was never rebuilt to 'A1X' configuration, as, after revenue service, it became the Brighton Works shunter as 'Loco Dept Brighton Works', then 'Loco Works Brighton' No 380s under the Southern Railway, by whom it was restored, apparently at Lancing. It was subsequently repaired and re-varnished by BR and in 1959/60 restored again at Eastleigh before moving to the erstwhile museum at Clapham, then on to York. As an aside, it never had a BR numberplate.

'So, we have here an 'A1X'. I believe it is one of three that were prepared at Eastleigh for display at Butlins Holiday Camps, the engines concerned being Nos (326)40 *Brighton*, (326)62

Martello and (326)78 *Knowle*. By this time in their lives, all had been converted to 'A1X' configuration with the smokebox on a saddle, a boiler with the dome moved forward from the original position, and extended Isle of Wight-type bunkers.

'This particular one has sandboxes below the footplate, so that eliminates the former *Brighton*. The only difference I can see is what I believe are exhaust steam domes (part of the Stroudley condensing apparatus associated with the copper pipes from smokebox to side tanks?) on the top of the tanks, which were removed from *Knowle*, presumably when sent to the Isle of Wight in 1929, whereas they were retained (and still are) by *Martello*. Colour-Rail has an image of *Martello* at Ayr Holiday Camp, and it clearly has this fitting, whereas Steamchest has a photograph of *Knowle* at Minehead without. It also retains its BR number plate, but the vacuum ejector pipe from cab front to smokebox has been removed as part of the 'restoration', presuming that it is now minus a vacuum brake? One further fitting in favour of *Knowle* is the presence of an additional front foot step, painted red in your photograph and retained at Minehead.

'There was one other 'A1' restored at Eastleigh, the former Lancing Works shunter DS680, formerly *Waddon*, which was presented to the Canadian Railway Historical Association in 1962. *Waddon* had retained an 'A1' smokebox with wing plates all of its life, but had latterly carried an 'A1X' boiler. The engine was restored at Eastleigh in 1963 and very creditable it looked before being shipped to Canada. But, only looking at photographs, I suspect it may still have an 'A1X' boiler with dome slightly further forward than original. Since I have never been to Canada, perhaps someone can tell us which boiler it has?

'That really is enough on 'Terriers' for one letter!'

Now from Nicholas Owen, who heads his comment with the word 'Gorging':

'A hiatus in getting *Southern Way* meant that I had to catch up and gorge myself on several issues in a few days. Wonderful. Brilliant contributions all round. A few comments of my own.

'The fascinating reference in 'SW32' by Charles Anderson to the Hythe and Sandgate horse tramway reminded me of tracing – with my dear pal and Southern Electric Group founder Tony Dyer – the remains of the Hellingly Hospital electric tramway in East Sussex. One traction pole buried in the woods complete with insulator made our day.

'Then, so many delights in Special Issue No 12, A Third-Rail Centenary, compiled by old friends from the SEG. So many interesting facts and photos. I'd make the point that coinciding with electrification to Brighton, the Southern Railway itself paid tribute in 1933 to the pioneering work of Volk's Railway, then celebrating its 50th anniversary, and of course operating with a third rail. It still does today and is about to benefit from a £1 million-plus grant from the Heritage Lottery Fund to upgrade stations and rolling stock. Do visit once seasonal operations begin again.' (I never have, but know I should – Ed)

'Finally, I was glad to see reference to a Class 73 loco being named *Sir Herbert Walker* after the Southern's great visionary General Manager. It was my great honour to do the actual

naming, at Selhurst depot back in the 1990s. Naively, I hoped the nameplate would be around as long as the loco itself. The switching and swapping of loco names deserves another article!'

Next from Chris Sayers-Leavy:

'I was very pleased that you published the piece by Harry Holcroft. I had seen some of the pictures before but was not aware of the background to the experiments or indeed much of the detail.

'I find this matter quite interesting on a number of levels, not the least of which was Maunsell's sanctioning of the project – as far as I am aware, he was not a great experimenter, although I am guessing that the potential savings were just too irresistible to be ignored. I am also not aware of any other UK railway loco engineers attempting a similar 'complete recovery' of the steam that has been generated for traction use, but it may just be that I am not aware.

'I am afraid that these comments have also progressed into a bit of a treatise...

'I am familiar with various loco classes (LBSCR 'Terrier', 'Met' tanks and GWR pannier tanks, for example) that were built as 'condensing engines', or perhaps better stated as 'engines with a partial condensing capability' – but other than for some late engines built for use in Africa, I don't think that the other UK efforts attempted such a complete recovery of the steam that a railway engine had produced before. Most of the other UK 'condensing' engines suffered from limitations associated with the returned feed water being too hot/of limited condensing capability and the problems of getting injectors to work with hot water.

'Having said all that, and not wishing to be a 'clever clogs' well after the event, it does not really surprise me that the venture came to nothing, for a number of reasons. These were not really detailed by Holcroft et al and I will explain my reasoning below.

'Going back to basics, one of the early things that I learned in my career on the UK railways is that, in many cases, railway engineering is a 'special case'. This is not that the principles are different in any way – rather more it is the way in which they were used in the railway environment. I have had this statement decried by many outsiders coming into the rail industry before – and yet virtually to a man they have had to learn the lesson the hard way, as they were just not prepared to be told. What I am referring to here is the very limited space that is available within the standard UK loading gauge, and the maximum axle loads that can be tolerated, etc; then there is the consideration as to what happens to a loco in use – variable loadings and speed on the track, i.e. the vibration, the various forces arising, the effect of wind and even entering tunnels, together with the vital ability to be able to see where you are going, etc, etc. Within reason anything in engineering is possible given enough space and freedom from external forces ... but to try and 'shoehorn' all of this into the UK loading gauge becomes a whole new ballgame. The foregoing alone, for me, should have been the first indication that trying to match the savings demonstrated in a stationary installation was not going to be easy, let alone successful.

'Various forms of 'economisers' were possible (and indeed developed and used) in marine installations (not really referred to by Holcroft), no doubt occasioned as much by the need for clean and fresh boiler water at sea, as much as a desire to improve efficiency. So it should not be any surprise that the ideas arose in the mind of an ex-marine engineering draughtsman. Neither should we be surprised at the savings being achieved in a stationary steam generation plant – but as soon as a railway application is considered, other factors come to bear, some of which I have yet to mention…

'I learned at a very young age how revolutionary the *Rocket* had been when compared to the other efforts that had been around at the time it was built. But what I did not appreciate at that young age is just what an understatement 'revolutionary' was. Others had tinkered around before Stephenson, in some cases for many years, but in the *Rocket* design most of the major principles of railway steam engine design were established that went right through to everything that followed to the end of steam haulage in the UK.

'Now, I'm going to be a bit anecdotal here, but what follows brought everything into perspective for me…

'Some of my early days in railway preservation were spent on the (original) Dart Valley line. A group of businessmen supported by an enthusiasts' association had reopened the line from Totnes (Riverside) to Buckfastleigh, intending to reach Ashburton. GWR steam haulage – no surprise there. I'm not sure of their original intention here – but it was probably the cost and transport involved in getting steam coal down to South Devon – but one of the directors had a 'tie-up' of some kind with Shell – the oil refinery people – and the idea arose as to whether or not oil-firing could be used on the line. This was fashionable at the time as the Ffestiniog was converting some of its engines – and it was also seen as a fire risk reduction measure (no hot ash/cinders being released). So an engineer was dispatched from Shell to come and see what would be required by such a scheme. The engineer joined the loco after steam had been raised, then travelled on the footplate down the line making observations on what would be required to fire the boiler. The trip (basically all downhill) was uneventful and at Totnes the engine ran round the train and started back up the branch to Buckfastleigh.

As the line climbed up the valley, the driver opened up the regulator – and the Shell engineer's jaw dropped at what was happening in the firebox. The firehole doors were rattling as the engine got into its stride; the blast from the exhaust steam lifted the fire and of course the boiler responded accordingly

This recently unearthed view of No A816 is of interest for several reasons. While similar to that seen on page 60 of 'SW33' and clearly also taken in the Eastleigh Paint Shop, this is the opposite, right-hand side of the engine. Now compare this view with that on page 60 of 'SW34', and it is immediately clear that, with its position in both views adjacent to the wall, it would imply that the Paint Shop was in fact where it was stored when not in use. In the earlier illustration referred to, the point is made that it was then possibly stored awaiting a decision as to its future. However, this may not now be the case, as clearly it was moved and, when returned, appeared facing the other way. Conclusion? Well, one of the views probably does show it pending its fate (neither is dated), and the other must then show it 'between trials' – but of course, which one? (Now all we need are some photographs of it actually on test!) Finally, compare the back wall with the views of the Eastleigh railway museum seen earlier…

and produced more steam. This was more than the chap from Shell could cope with – he had never seen anything like it before, being used to static oil-fired boilers, and had never seen the effect that the blast pipe/exhaust steam had on a coal fire, promptly declaring that they had nothing to match the response time of the 'blast on the fire' with oil-firing. He promptly gave up trying to come up with an oil-firing solution. This brought Stephenson's achievements into focus for me.

(Without wishing in any way to contradict Chris, we know that there had been several reasonably successful oil-firing conversions on the railways before this time, on the GWR perhaps mostly, but the SR had also achieved positive results with several types of steam engine converted to oil fuel in the late 1940s. Unfortunately this expertise was not available to the man from Shell in the late 1960s – Ed)

'Now I mention the foregoing for two reasons. The first is the perfect demonstration of what we would now call a 'control feedback loop' – and it could not be any simpler. In one fell swoop, intentionally or not, Stephenson had come up with a near perfect control system for ensuring that the driver had a supply of steam to match the demands that the engine (cylinders) placed on the boiler. It is a little bit more complicated than my brief description, but the basic layout of separate firebox, multi-flue fire-tube boiler and exhaust steam blast pipe formed the basic blueprint for virtually all of the railway steam engines to be built thereafter. The second reason why I mention this is because the developments on No A816 effectively removed the 'control feedback loop' and this is so critical in ensuring a 'load matching' performance from the boiler. I know that they left the blast pipe in place – but the intention was not to use it other than for starting trains.

'Personally I think that the idea/influence came from Stephenson's early days at the blacksmith's forge – where a similar effect can be seen on the fire from an air blast from the bellows – but there are others to whom historians also attribute the idea; nevertheless, it was Stephenson who made it into a practical working system.

'The boiler on a steam loco has two main functions. It is a steam generator, and also a stored reserve of energy, actually containing a lot more stored energy than its physical size would suggest, partly because of the expansive characteristic of steam and also because it contains a large volume of water that is 'contained' at a temperature above that at which it would normally boil. This is a very attractive characteristic, as it means that, as steam is drawn off without any further heating, steam continues to be produced as the water boils. This is the principle used in 'fireless' locos, and allows a conventional steam loco to have a reserve of power that is instantly available. Clearly it is desirable to replace quickly the used stored energy in the boiler – and this is where the effect of the blast pipe on the fire comes in. All these features allow for the building of a very compact power plant, which can then be put on wheels! Another, but indirectly related, characteristic of a steam engine is that the maximum power is available when it starts its motion and no complicated gear boxes are required as in a road vehicle.

'I have very respect for my forbearers, particularly Harry Holcroft and perhaps to a lesser extent Maunsell – they were both better engineers that I will ever be – but they seemed to get seriously side-tracked by chasing the attractive savings on the A816 loco developments.

'How on earth did the issue with the fan rotating the wrong way get missed until a live steam trial of the completed machine? Was the small engine that drove it not reversible? I would have expected the fan to have been tried before the engine was steamed, either on compressed air or via a steam line. Then there is the matter of the fan blades; this type of fan is normally made up of individual blades mounted on a central boss and the fan can be assembled with different numbers of blade/blade pitches. It is not that easy to tell from the picture on page 55, but the blades in the picture on page 56 are not of any aerofoil section – i.e. they are just flat blades, so the fan should have been reversible, either by running it in the opposite direction or by just taking it off and turning it round, with the same performance.

'Then there is the matter of the performance of the fan in moving the fire/smokebox gases (even Holcroft admits that this was through a tortuous route). I have reasonable experience of motor-driven fans of various kinds and this type performs best at a constant speed, so how did they ever expect it to match the performance of the blast pipe on the fire? I realise that part of the attraction was to stop 'fire throwing', something that has to be seen to be believed – have you ever seen a steam engine working hard at night without any other light pollution – i.e. in total darkness? The show is to say the least spectacular and you are left wondering why everything behind the train isn't alight!

'In my view fan draughting of a fire-tube boiler would work OK in a static installation where the steam demands on the boiler are fairly constant and even peak demands could be met, given sufficient reserve capacity in the boiler to allow time for the response to take place, but I don't believe that the demands occasioned by a loco driver opening up the regulator or increasing the cut-off significantly when it came to negotiating a major gradient/recovering from a signal stop, etc, could be tackled by fan draughting alone. The effect on the fire of the exhaust blast is so quick that more heat is produced as soon as the steam demand goes up, whereas with a fan there is always going to be a lag in getting the fan moving faster and livening up the fire. Hence the easy reversion back to using the blast pipe, but there would still be a delay either way, suggesting that the driver/fireman would have to pre-empt the steam demand, before it actually occurred, in order to stay on top of managing the boiler properly.

'Holcroft appears to suggest that the effect of the exhaust steam passing through the blast pipe and lifting the fire is undesirable, and this surprises me. Yes, 'fire throwing' needs to be eliminated where possible, but this is part of the feedback loop, the same feedback loop that gives the rapid response to steam being drawn off from the boiler. Such a blast is not required on a stationary plant with a chain grate in the firebox, but in a steam loco the lifting of the fire in the grate

Tooley Street, along the north side of and adjacent to London Bridge station – notice the poster board on the right-hand wall – is viewed looking towards Tower Bridge Road at 2.30pm on Monday 1 March 1937, and while the motor lorry is now well-established, there are at least three 'horsepower' drays still present.

greatly assists the air flow to the fire through the dampers and can help to stop clinker forming into a solid mass.

'Then there is the matter of managing the boiler water level, which Holcroft does not really address. No matter how perfect the installation is, there will still be the need for some external water to be added to the boiler, to make up for the water used by the condensation pumps and fan motor alone. Again, little is said about actually returning the condensate back into the boiler, but the speed of the pumps would have to match the rate of condensing (hence the boiler feed pump was driven by the condenser engine), and this in turn would be dependent on the rate that exhaust steam is being produced, but little is said about how this would be regulated, as the diagrams are only 'schematic'.

'Early steam locos used motion-driven pumps to replace the water that had been used as steam, but this quickly became as much of a hazard as it was a benefit. Shortage of boiler feed water going into the boiler leads inevitably to some form of catastrophic failure and there are tales of engines having to be run up against buffer stops, etc, and the rails being oiled to enable the engine to run in order get water into the boiler! Steam-driven feed water pumps were introduced to overcome this problem, but they use steam and require maintenance whereas injectors were so much simpler.

'Now in the middle of all the effort to recover the steam that has been used for traction, there is also the matter of the water vapour being released to atmosphere from the condensers … and this is where I have difficulty trying to understand why Messrs Holcroft and Maunsell thought that all the effort involved with the installation would be so worthwhile. Were they so railway-focused that they could not see the obvious differences between a fixed/stationary set-up and what would be required to get it to work charging along the track? For me, as soon as you have to expend yet more energy trying to recover what has already been used you are on a hiding to nothing … it is only now, with electric traction, that we are starting to see the benefits of energy recovery on the railways – something that they had the genesis of 100 years ago, but failed to take seriously. And no other organisation was better suited than the Southern Railway to develop this – indeed, an historical lost opportunity. Furthermore, the advent of the National Grid – providing somewhere to 'dump' your recovered electrical energy (which of course you would be paid for) other than powering other trains – opened up a whole plethora of new possibilities, and the LBSCR OLE system would have been ideally suited to do this! Conversely, the use of the LSWR third-rail system effectively negated this option – although of course it is a lot easier on the eye.

'In respect of Holcroft's conclusion – 'What might have been?' – I'm afraid that I don't think that the proposals would have fared much better. I agree with your summation that the plans were just an idea, with the protagonists knowing that there was no chance of them being progressed. There are so many things here that seem a bit 'iffy' to me.

'I get the link between the chimney fan and the use of live steam, but there would still be a lag in the effect it would have on the boiler, and perhaps the prestigious performance of the Bulleid boiler might have reduced the significance of this. But hang on a moment – I thought that the Bulleid firebox was designed to get the maximum out of poor coal – which would have plenty of contaminants in it – thus relying on the blast to keep the fire 'free'. Leaving this aside, as soon as you start converting energy – a small turbine driving a generator – there are additional losses, particularly on a small-scale installation, so I'm sorry but I think that it was just too complicated to be of any real benefit. Then there was the matter of the condensers, pumps, etc, being under the casing. Were they really serious – had they not learned anything? Personally I'm surprised that Holcroft went along with these ideas; Bulleid I can understand, but I would have thought better of Holcroft.

'Lastly, the suggestion of using a steam/electrically driven exhauster. I cannot understand the logic of this – it is just an unnecessary complication almost just for the sake of it. Holcroft had been at Swindon and one of the Churchward innovations that always impressed me was the effectiveness of his crosshead-driven vacuum pumps. Once vacuum has been created and the train is in motion, the crosshead pump very effectively maintains the vacuum, uses the minimum of addition steam, and the inertia of the train keeps it going – simplicity at its best. You still need an ejector to create the initial vacuum, but this is not used again after starting.

'Like it or not, steam locos as we know them are 'total loss' machines. Nothing is easily recovered, whether it is heat, steam/water or oil; it is all expended in creating the effort. Bulleid had a go at conserving oil – another nice idea, let down perhaps by the materials on hand at the time, but still difficult to do even today.

'Steam railway locos are in fact very simple machines, which ensured their longevity, relatively low construction costs, ease of manufacture and use, etc, etc, and for your outlay you got a very powerful machine. All the time that coal and labour was cheap and plentiful and environmental pollution was not a serious consideration, steam locos were bound to thrive, but essentially they were and still are a Victorian invention that has not changed significantly in over 120 years.'

Clearly this is a subject on which Chris has profound feelings as, shortly after receiving the above, he continued the theme:

'Hi, Kevin, I'm still musing on the Holcroft article in 'SW33', and wondered if the following observations would be of any use to you.

'Why do we sometimes not see any exhaust steam being released from a moving steam engine?

'Holcroft made an interesting comment at the beginning of his article relating to the above matter, when he said that 'Those travelling by train are all familiar with the sight of white clouds of steam rolling across the countryside arising from exhaust ejected from the chimney of the locomotive, though in this era of superheat it is not so frequently to be seen as in days gone by.'

'From the earliest days of locomotive railway haulage, the path of a train could be seen from a distance across the countryside as the engine released a steady stream of clouds of white 'steam' as it progressed along the line. The steam that was seen is in fact vaporised water similar to that which we see when a kettle is boiling. Water vapour consists of water that is in a halfway state between a liquid and a gas, and consists of lots of small water droplets that quickly condense back into water as soon as the temperature of the steam is reduced. This phenomenon is easily seen in the domestic situation in kitchens and bathrooms, where water droplets in the air condense back into water as soon as they touch something cold, e.g. glazed tiles, single-glazed windows and items of metalwork, sometimes the incoming cold water supply pipe, although this is less so in the 21st century with the increasing use of plastic piping. The hotter the steam, the longer it takes to lose its latent heat and condense back into water vapour, then water again.

'Water is a very interesting liquid, being made up (as we were taught at school) from two gases – two parts hydrogen and one part oxygen by volume – the familiar H_2O chemical formula. However, unlike most other liquids water actually expands as it freezes (hence burst pipes, etc), and when it is heated its vapour expands some 400 times its original volume. When it turns into steam it is this expansive nature that makes it so ideal and convenient as a source of stored energy, such as to power a steam engine.

'Energy storage in a steam locomotive takes two forms: 1) the quantity of water contained within the boiler that cannot actually boil at its normal boiling point due to the pressure of its containment, and 2) the expansive nature of the steam once it is drawn off from the boiler. As with the water in the boiler, the steam is contained under pressure and during this containment its temperature can be raised still further, greatly increasing its expansive quality, which is the purpose of the 'superheater'. Steam that is drawn direct from the boiler is called saturated steam, i.e. it is a mixture of steam and water vapour. If the saturated steam is then taken back through the burning gases (in the boiler fire tubes) that are being given off by the fire, it can then be heated further until it becomes 'dry steam' or truly water in a gaseous state without any water vapour in it – and this is invisible to the observer.

'Superheated steam has even more stored energy in it than that which is released when saturated steam expands. The 'expansion' takes place in the cylinders and it is controlled by the position of the valve gear in relation to the pistons. Shutting off the steam supply to the cylinder halfway through the piston's stroke allows the steam to continue to expand as it moves the piston along the cylinder. This action is known as increasing the 'cut-off' and the driver is able to control the amount of 'cut-off' that is used in order to reduce the amount of steam being used and conversely not waste any more steam than is necessary for the 'effort' he needs to apply in order to move the train along the track (tractive effort).

'Another interesting feature of a simple steam locomotive is that the maximum tractive effort is available at the point of

The three-cylinder Maunsell 'Mogul', in the form of (right) 'U1' No 31901 and (left) two-cylinder 'N' No 31831, at Ashford. Something in the right background may also be of note – part of a cab sheet numbered '...4012'. So where was No 34012 *Launceston* at this time? Presumably under repair. Certainly those are Bulleid wheels in the foreground.

starting (assuming that full boiler pressure is available), and it is limited only by the engine's ability to grip the rail – as it is just a simple 'friction drive' arrangement. This is very different from other forms of traction where the use of a high-power source (diesel engine/electric motor) can only be applied for rail traction through the use of some form of gearing to reduce the speed of the power source such that it can be applied to a stationary railway wheel. This gearing, be it electrical or mechanical, and the associated cost of making and maintaining it, are all extra costs that are not required in the manufacture of a steam engine.

'But to return to the matter of 'superheating'. It is only available when there is sufficient temperature in the burning firebox gases to further raise the temperature of the saturated steam. So on a locomotive it is saturated steam that is available to start the train's motion. However, once the train is on the move and the blast from the exhaust steam passing through the blast pipe orifice/smokebox draws yet more air through the fire, the temperature of the fire is raised and with it there is an increase in the rate that combustible gases are 'driven off' from the coal. It is these gases that contain the real stored energy in the coal, and they pass over the brick arch and into the boiler fire tubes as they burn, thus raising the temperature within the fire tubes and a) passing some of the heat into the boiler water and b) passing over the superheater elements where the superheated steam is produced. The superheated steam is then gathered in the superheater 'header' before it is passed to the cylinders, where the expansion is subsequently converted into rotary motion of the driving wheels.

'The effect of superheated steam to the passenger is not readily apparent. The effect to the observer of a passing train is that when an engine is using 'superheated' steam the white clouds from the chimney can no longer be seen. This is because the exhaust steam leaving the chimney no longer contains any water vapour. Unfortunately, all of the stored energy released from the coal is of course just wasted once the steam is released to the atmosphere, and it was this that made the developments tried on loco No A816 such an attractive proposition.

'The place to see the effects of superheating in action is on the footplate of the locomotive! However, on today's preserved steam-hauled railways I doubt very much whether any of the engines are worked sufficiently hard for the firebox temperatures to became high enough to start the superheating process, but it should occur in engines used for main-line running. One of the best examples that can be seen of an engine superheating is via the internet at https://www.youtube.com/watch?v=vDVoYVM-60, between 1.10 and 1.30, comprising some footage of *Duke of Gloucester* running at speed. Sounding more like a sewing machine than a steam loco, and with just a light blue haze coming from the chimney, the fireman has a good fire and the engine is superheating – with no discernible exhaust steam.

'When superheating starts, it is a bit like finding a fifth gear when you have only been used to having four in a car – the engine takes on a new persona and just wants to run and run. In fact, the only time that I saw it in action, the driver had some difficulty managing the engine – as the cut-off was wound back

further and further, so the engine just wanted to keep going (this was No 4555 with the fully loaded Chipman's weedkiller train non-stop from Totnes Riverside to Ashburton). It might only have been a small engine, but I was very impressed with what it could do once it started superheating. It had been arranged to spray the line as an extra part of the train's regular visit to South Devon, and the trip had a very tightly time 'window' to get the train back to Totnes to pick up on the rest of its planned workings. After running up to Ashburton (still open back then) and having climbed for most of the way, they then sprayed the line on the return journey – after they managed to quieten the engine down to avoid the risk of running out of water on the loco! As I recall it (but not that well, I'm afraid), I think that there were two coaches, three loaded four-wheel tanks, a handful of box vans full of the necessary chemicals, and maybe a brake van.

'The fireman (an ex-Nine Elms man) knew how to shovel, and the fire was no longer an orangey yellow in colour, but incandescent white. Even using the shovel as a shield, you could not look at the fire as it was so bright, and the boiler just kept steaming. The engine dug into the task at hand and the injectors were singing, an experience that (as it was some 47 years ago) I am not likely to witness again. In fact, the most difficult task of all was keeping the engine quiet and the boiler under control. No wonder some of the traffic departments shunned the diesels when they came in, as they could not hold a candle to a steam loco in good condition, with good steam coal and a good crew.

'These days, reviewers of black & white pictures of steam engines working will see many images where they are churning out great clouds of the dark and dirty 'clag' so beloved by photographers. But this is not the reality. In many cases (and even still today) photographers arrange for the crew to present such a display just for the picture. However, a steam engine that is in good order and with a crew that is on top of the job actually produces very little obvious visual pollution. Don't get me wrong here – engines do produce ash/cinders and sulphur and carbon, all ejected through the chimney, and of course much of the poor coal that was used in later years resulted in poor steaming, over-firing and excessive clinker being produced in the attempt to just keep things going.

'So towards the end of steam, that which the enthusiasts liked to see actually just gave the critics/modernisers all the evidence they needed to bring about the change to other forms of traction.'

Moving on, we received an email from George Hobbs on the subject of 'SW24', page 59:

'The picture of the brand new D65xx looks to me as though it is coming off the Chatham Loop, from the south end of Chislehurst station, leading down to the LCDR main line at St Mary Cray Junction. I believe the first examples were shedded at Hither Green, so my guess is that this is a test run from there. At the time I lived in Chislehurst, so this was definitely home territory!'

Apropos pigeons, yes, I know this is not on the Southern, but the vans are similar to those referred to by Neil. This is pigeon release at Selby in August 1953. *R. Blencowe*

Now from Neil Knowlden:

'Another fascinating issue (No 34), and before I even read through it properly there were a few things to comment on. On page 23 it is interesting to see a 'Dub-Dee' 2-10-0 (Riddles 'WD' type) in use on the Southern, well away from Eastleigh where they were refurbished before transfer to Scotland.

'On page 28, though commonly known as Ashford West, this was probably never an official name, as the LCDR station went out of use when the working union was instigated.

'Page 31 lower and page 36 upper, surely these were pigeon specials too (from the vans)? (I would concur – Ed)

'On page 35, No E68000 most certainly wasn't built for the Kent Coast Electrification; it was a one-off for Tyneside (the 'E' prefix is a clue). I'd guess the picture shows it on trial before it headed north. Unfortunately it didn't have the traction batteries of the (what later became) Class 419s so couldn't join them when Tyneside was short-sightedly de-electrified. Instead it seems to have disappeared to Merseyside for a few years (see http://www.bloodandcustard.com/mlv001.html). As it had two motor bogies, the Southern could then have used it as a depot shunter somewhere – but, obviously, that didn't happen and it went for the chop appropriately at Willoughby Choppington.

'Page 37 upper, at first sight this is a partially or fully fitted freight, but how many 'pillbox' brakes were through-piped at this date?

'Page 42 – do I get a prize for saying Wadhurst and Ashey?

'On page 61 the 'S15s' you refer to had 4,000-gallon six-wheel tenders – later in life one of the other 'S15s' was coupled to a 3,500-gallon one like this and the footplate mis-match was very conspicuous. No, this is an 'N15' (from Nos 793 to 806, though No 802 on page 64 was one of three of this batch that has gained a bogie tender by this date – five more followed.

'On page 62 sets 471 and 472 are the only candidates, as the others were standard Maunsell stock and a number had been disbanded already. No sets numbered 473/4 seem to have existed. David Gould remarks that 'Nos 471/2 were

special traffic sets berthed on the Eastern Section in the 1950s, and both withdrawn in 1959.'

Whichever set is illustrated, it's been augmented with so many mis-matched loose vehicles that it's impossible to reconcile it with the theoretical formation – 471 ran with a Maunsell brake at on end from 1946 – but your guess is as good as mine what's at the London end of this lot!

'Page 76, the 'Light Pacifics' with plain rods in preservation probably 'borrowed' 'Merchant Navy' sets before leaving Barry scrapyard.

'On page 80, I'm afraid it was only 'Special' cattle that travelled in vans – yer bovine hoi polloi had to make do with ordinary cattle trucks!

'Page 91, etc – I've always wondered why the Lullingstone Airport site wasn't developed as a fighter base when the war postponed civilian proposals. Maybe it was just too obvious and a 'dummy' airfield was thought a better option?'

Next from Nowak Pawel:

'Alan Postlethwaite's fascinating selection of freight photographs in *Southern Way* No 34 brings back some distant memories. In the case of the top illustration on page 35, the 'ex-works' condition of the MLV suggests the kind of 'running-in turn' familiar to observers of unusual steam workings. As all new BR EMU construction had been concentrated at Eastleigh by this time, with no adjacent third rail, some testing was carried out on the Brighton main line, with certain freight reception lines and sidings conveniently equipped with third rail (and in places 750V overhead tram line) electrification for use in freight traffic by No 20001 and her sister locomotives, as shown in the lower photograph.

'The unusual feature here is the non-SR front-end design and the vehicle number (E68000), which betray its intended use on the Tyneside electrified network to replace or supplement equivalent vehicles inherited from the LNER. When a later decision not to renew the traction power supply forced the re-equipment of the Tyneside network by four-car Metro-Cammell DMUs, this MLV (which seems have been referred to as an MPV up north) and its almost-new passenger-carrying stablemates based on the 2-EPB design migrated south. Unlike those intended for the Victoria-Folkestone/Dover boat trains, this vehicle appears to have no battery compartment and so made it unsuitable for use on the quaysides with inset 'tram tracks' where no electrification could be installed. Hence it is reported to have ended a comparatively short life on the Liverpool-Southport line, whereas the 2-EPBs lasted till the adoption of sliding-door stock on SR suburban services.

'The freight train being hauled appears fairly light by modern standards, but could still be up to 200 tons depending on the contents (if any) of the wagons. What is uncertain here is the proportion of vacuum-fitted wagons, as the contribution to the total brake force of an MLV must have been very small compared to a locomotive. All freight trains would have had a brake van at this time, so that in itself does not denote a partially fitted train, and the pale colours of some of the open wagons in a black & white photograph may not necessarily have been the grey reserved for unfitted vehicles. The ability to operate simultaneously in EPB and vacuum brake mode was one of the clever features of the MLV, hence the need to test its ability to pull a small but worthwhile load, usually in normal service made up of vacuum-braked parcels vans.' (Others have passed similar comment on this MLV/NPV, for which we are grateful – Ed)

Now some information on our frontispiece image in SW34 from Greg Beecroft:

'This shows the subway under Crystal Palace Parade (the road on the east side of the high-level station), linking the station and Crystal Palace. It was at a higher level than the high-level station, not below it. I think it was accessed from a footbridge over the platforms.'

And from Ross Woollard:

'I was fascinated by many of the photographs in *Southern Way* 34 and would like to comment on three of them, two of which are dated on the Bluebell Railway Photographic Archive website.

'First, the photograph of No 90766 on a down freight train at East Croydon on page 23. The 'WD' 2-10-0s were exceedingly rare on the Southern Region during their working lives as they spent virtually all their time in BR service on the Scottish Region. The Bluebell Photographic Archive tells us that the photograph was taken on 18.6.49, and contemporary railway enthusiast periodicals provide the background to the loco's appearance at East Croydon. No 90766 (as 'WD' No 77390) went into Brighton Works for overhaul during the period 2.1.49-17.2.49 (March 1949 *Railway Observer*). *Railway Locomotives* (the journal of the British Locomotive Society) in its May/June 1949 issue reported it as being in Brighton Works on 26.2.49. It was seen on Brighton motive power depot on 15.6.49, three days before the photograph was taken (July 1949 *Stephenson Locomotive Society Journal*), and the August

1949 issue stated that it was renumbered 90766 in June. Its first BR allocation was to Motherwell in the week-ending 9.7.49, so it was presumably borrowed by Brighton or another SR shed for a short time before going to Scotland.

'Second, regarding the photograph of an unidentified 'S15' on page 61, the caption states that it must have been one of Nos (30)833-837. If so, the engine was well off its beaten track at St Mary Cray, as those five were always allocated to sheds on the Western or Central Sections. However, in Southern Railway days Nos 838-841 were allocated to Hither Green from new in 1936, with No 842 joining them there from Feltham in 1937. They all moved away from the Eastern Section in October 1939. I wonder if the loco could have been one of the Hither Green engines – a tender swap perhaps?

'Lastly, the photograph of No 31838 on page 37; looking very smart, the view was taken on Saturday 9 May 1953 between Canterbury West and Ashford. I assume this loco was running in after a visit to Ashford Works (confirmed as it was reported as in Ashford Works on 25.4.53, again according to *Railway Locomotives* for June 1953) and, like No 90766, it lacks a shed plate. East Kent trainspotters would have been delighted to see it, as it was allocated to Exmouth Junction throughout its BR existence!'

Moving away from 'SW' briefly and to Mike King's 2016 book *Southern Rolling Stock in Colour*, Trevor Davis comments:

'I recently bought a copy of this wonderful tome and can add a little information. This book includes a photo (page 119) of brake van No S56304 at Romford. I visited Romford Coal Yard with the late Graham Taylor (a Romford resident) on 17 July 1977 and there were two vans present, Nos 56302 and 56304, duly photographed by us. Graham also visited on 25 July, when only No 56302 was photographed. I was led to believe that the vans were used mainly on the brewery siding, which ran under and at right angles to the main line. Incidentally, the yard track included some on GER chairs, one of which I recorded.'

Finally for this issue, some further notes on the signalling at Calstock (SW34) from Roger Whitehouse:

'The statements about signalling in the captions on page 71 of issue 34 are not correct. Calstock was a block post. George Pryer (*Signal Box Diagrams of the Great Western and Southern Railways*, Volume 13, page 56) states that Calstock's signal box was opened in 1908. The Southern Railway's 'Extracts from Block Regulations etc for Drivers, Firemen and Guards' dated 2 February 1930 show Bere Alston-Calstock worked by train staff and ticket, and Calstock-Gunnislake by electric train tablet (changed to electric key token in the Working Timetable dated 8 June 1953). From 12 February 1951, or possibly earlier, on Mondays to Fridays the engine of the 4.53pm Plymouth Friary-Bere Alston and 6.01pm Bere Alston-Gunnislake ran light to Bere Alston to work the 8.00pm Bere Alston-Callington, crossing the 7.10pm Bere Alston-Callington at Calstock, and this pattern of working continued until after the final transfer to the Western Region in 1963.'

Forgotten Railways
The Greenwich Park Branch

On 23 May 1929 Edward Wallis visited the remains of the branch, recording images at Lewisham Road, Blackheath Hill and Greenwich Park. Wallis notes that we see the remains of Lewisham Road viewed looking westwards (towards Nunhead), taken from a brake van standing on the up line. The former station building and platform are on the right. The down line is original track, while the up line has been relaid with new fittings. To the right are the earthworks for the new connection to St Johns opened in the same year.

On 18 September 1871 the London, Chatham & Dover Railway opened the first section of its new Greenwich branch from Nunhead and the junction of the Crystal Palace Line as far as Blackheath Hill. The line was eventually completed through to the new terminus at Greenwich (the suffix 'Park' was added in 1900) on 1 October 1888. There was no rail connection with the existing 1838 station at Greenwich on the South Eastern Railway's North Kent line.

Although intended to challenge the SER for traffic from Greenwich into London, the new route was to say the least tortuous, and instead found its niche as a leisure destination serving Greenwich Park and, in the opposite direction, accommodating those from Greenwich wishing to visit the Crystal Palace.

There matters might have rested until the introduction of road trams in the area in 1908 saw a rapid decline in receipts. Prior to this there were, according to Prof H. P. White, no fewer than fifty-seven down trains in 1904, many of them shuttle services from the terminus to Nunhead. In an attempt to restore revenue, the SECR (the LCDR and SER had amalgamated in 1899, hence also the name change referred to above, intended to avoid confusion between the two stations) introduced a push-pull operation in 1913, which by August of the following year had risen to a regular 20-minute-interval peak-hour service and 45 minutes during off-peak times.

Services continued thus until 1 January 1917 when, it was stated, 'as an economy measure' the branch was closed. On the same date an identical fate befell the Crystal Palace line from Nunhead.

After the war, the Crystal Palace line was reopened in 1919, but not so that to Greenwich Park. Instead, the railway was operated as far as Brockley Lane for goods and thence to Lewisham Road for carriage storage (both these stations were between Nunhead and Blackheath Hill). The portion thence from Lewisham Road through Blackheath Hill to Greenwich Park lay moribund.

In 1927 the Southern Railway refurbished the section from Nunhead as far as Lewisham Road, at the same time providing a connection from St Johns and Lewisham, which opened two years later on 7 July 1929. This section as far as Nunhead was electrified in 1935, although the intermediate stations were not reopened for passenger traffic. Meanwhile the moribund final section from the new connection through Blackheath Hill to Greenwich Park was formally abandoned in 1929.

At Blackheath Hill station another signal arm is still present. The archway in the distance was the start of a 150-yard covered way between here and the terminus. Facilities for passengers included a substantial canopy on the up platform (towards Nunhead), but there was no provision on the opposite platform – there would be few passengers travelling the short distance from here to the terminus. Following closure, the station building became a billiard hall but was substantially altered some time afterwards, being used by a light engineering firm. Since 1987 the site has given way to housing.

On the same date, track had been recovered from the approach to Blackheath Hill (from Lewisham Road) although the down distant still proclaimed 'clear'. Notice the Coligny-Welch lamp.

Looking in the opposite direction it is perhaps surprising to find the running-in board still in position, while rails lengths await recovery.

This is Greenwich Park from what had once been the engine siding. Again there is a surviving signal arm. Clearly Edward Wallis had arrived at a time when anything potentially reusable or with some value was in the process of being recovered. The station signal box had been located close to where the photograph was taken from.

The terminus had boasted three platform faces and an engine release road in the middle of the two platforms seen.

Finally, looking from the buffer stops, recovery of bricks may be seen, while at least four men are also at work. Notice too the engine pit in the centre road. Following closure, the platforms were buried and in the 1920s the substantial main building was being used as the Mayfield Temperance Billiard Hall. Some time after this it was used by a timber merchant until it was demolished around 1968; the site is now a hotel and the former platform area the hotel car park.

*

As I was in the process of preparing this article news came through of the passing of David Wallis. David and I had discussed this very article only a short time before he died; although he never saw the proof, it is still included as a tribute to him. I had been aware of the Wallis collection of images for some years and on my first meeting with David it was necessary to convince him of my 'bona fides' following, as he put it, 'a bad experience a few years before'. The result was three books, *Southern Infrastructure*, a second book with a similar title, and a third volume on the Great Western. It was always a pleasure to speak to him; when visiting you expected cold tea – he would venture off into the kitchen but then get distracted! David was a man who, because of his lifetime of railway experience, was knowledgeable in most areas. A former railwayman, he later became involved with the Bluebell, particularly with his favourite topic – signalling. It was both a pleasure and a privilege to have known David Wallis, and I am sure readers will join me in passing on condolences to his family.

Southern Blue

Like it or not, 'green became blue' from the mid-1960s onwards. Personally I recall the first time I saw a set in all-over blue when a brand-new* 'TC' set appeared one morning on a test trip behind what we then knew as a 'D65' – others called them 'Cromptons' and they now go by the name Class 33.

It would be wrong to state a preference one way or the other for the actual livery – such issues are purely to personal taste and surely it was what was inside that mattered. Later, of course, on rolling stock at least, 'blue' became 'blue and grey' while aluminium embellishments such as window surrounds either disappeared or were painted over. Change can indeed be subtle.

While this may be the last feature in this issue, I should also refer to the first – the Editorial – where I question how much more we should duplicate steam 'history'; after all, the Southern was also a major electric railway. This fact was brought home to me by one of my regular research assistants, Nigel Barnes-Evans (every so often Nigel will send across something totally unexpected but worthwhile), whose own Southern interest does perhaps veer towards the blue era. So for this piece a slight change. Do let me know what you think – more or less of the same? After all, what is seen in the next few pages is also now history.

Above: Out to grass for the last time, 2BIL No 2146 awaits dismantling. The location is not shown but has the 'Long Marston' feel about it. As yet there is no vandalism and it may well be that it has only recently arrived, but is already being prepared for firing – then the quickest way of removing the bodywork so that the metal underframe may be cut up. No doubt it might also be a rich source of enthusiasts' 'souvenirs'.

Below: Almost looking tired and worn, and certainly dated by comparison with the 'CEP' or similar alongside, this is 2BIL set No 2025 at Portsmouth Harbour. I am sure a reader will correct me on this as necessary, but I am not sure if these sets ever went into 'blue/grey', or certainly if they did it was not all of them. Harbour station was literally where it said – at the harbour. The 750DC supply for the train from the third rail was of course used for heating and lighting within the set where necessary, but not on these early sets for the tail lamp, which continues to be lit by good old-fashioned paraffin oil. (I was tempted at this point to include a view of the preserved 2BIL unit No 2090 – that is until it was pointed out that the chosen view shows it in green, not 'Southern Blue'!)

* I appreciate that the 'TCs' were a rebuild of earlier Mark 1 stock.

Of the same vintage as the 2BIL sets were the 4COR type, built for the Southern's electrification extensions to Portsmouth and mid-Sussex in the 1930s. Despite many readers perhaps having a propensity for steam, I doubt if there will be many who do not also have a sneaking liking for these sets as well. Characterised as 'Nelsons' in view of their 'one-eyed' appearance (the left-hand window at the front was taken up by an indicator blind or, as here, towards the end of its life, with red shades), they certainly also lived up to their nickname with a gentle swaying motion – particularly on the faster stretches of the 'Portsmouth Direct', akin perhaps to being on a gentle sea swell. Mr Bulleid had fitted out some of the buffet cars in the similar 'RES' and 'BUF' sets as one of the first tasks when he had arrived on the Southern. Unfortunately he did it a little too well, as diners found them so comfortable that they did not want to leave, thus reducing the flow of revenue. According to the late John Click, that was one reason why Bulleid produced the seating portion of the later 'Tavern cars' without windows, to encourage diners not to linger, although Click admits that in this area he perhaps went a little too far. Set No 3135 is seen in its last days at Bognor.

Left: No snapshot of Southern EMUs (in blue) would be complete without a picture of the famed 'Brighton Belle'. The last of the 'Belle' trains of the Southern Region to remain in service, it is seen here in its final state in blue/grey (rather than the reversed Pullman livery then being used elsewhere). Hopefully this sight will soon be able to be recreated with the restoration of one set to running order.

Below: This is BR Blue (although 'blue and sliver' would be more accurate). Two of the Bulleid 'Waterloo & City' cars, fresh from overhaul and, it appears, repainting, await their move out of the daylight and back towards the bowels beneath Waterloo. This was the last truly Southern Railway stock to remain in public service and also the last Bulleid-design vehicles in operation.

After a lifetime underground, a new lease of life for some former LT Underground stock was found on the remaining electrified section of the Isle of Wight system. This is the terminus at Shanklin with a Ryde train awaiting departure. On the opposite set of rails years of accumulated oil and ash from the former steam services will take some time to disappear.

Right: For a time in the 1960s, certain Victoria to East Grinstead passenger workings were in the hands of SR diesel-electric units. Here a non-corridor 'Hampshire' unit leads a rake into Clapham Junction on such a working.

Below: The mainstay of the Southern inner-suburban services for several decades was the 'EPB' sets in either open or compartment form, the latter type intended for 'six-a-side' comfort…! In Network SouthEast days (note the red lamp posts), No 5176 appears freshly painted in BR Blue, and with the modern addition of a headlamp.

'Modern' main-line stock in the form of 4CIG No 7369 leads two other four-car units, all of which are electrically powered. These sets, together with the similar 'CEP' and 'BEP' units, were the replacements for the Southern Railway 'PAN', 'PUL' and 'CITY' design, and also shared a front-end design that was similar to the later 'TC' and 'REP' units. Blue and grey was probably a better combination than the original all-over blue, while the disadvantage with automatic carriage washers is apparent from the areas that the brushes were unable to reach.

Southern Region 4SUB unit No 4296 is seen in final form and also likely towards the end of its life. Following withdrawal, electric units were normally congregated at various electric depots where anything that might be salvaged was removed before the carcase was sold on for scrap. However, several of these 4SUB sets had a prolonged lease of life at Eastleigh, being used as a trailing load at the time when Class 56 diesel locomotives were being used for driver-training coupled to air-braked stock.

This is one of the two prototype 'PEP' units, Nos 4001 and 4002, which saw service on the Southern Region in the mid-1970s. Intended as a high-density replacement for existing suburban stock, internally they featured 2+2 seating with wide aisles. In consequence, and because of the high number of standing passengers that resulted on certain routes, the 'PEP' initials were soon corrupted as standing for 'Pack 'Em Perpendicular'. Being prototypes and featuring unique features, they were unable to run in multiple with other Southern Region stock and were therefore destined for a short life, being withdrawn as early as May 1977. However, in that time they did yield valuable information and were the basis of the design for subsequent batches of both AC and DC units on the Southern Region and elsewhere. (With grateful thanks to Colin Duff for information.)

No view of Southern EMUs would be complete without at least a glimpse of one of the two unique 'double-deck' sets, No 4901, formerly No 4001, on its regular Dartford run complete with 70 headcode. Here was a valiant attempt (Mr Bulleid of course) at providing more seats but with the same length of train. In theory it worked, although the disadvantage was the dwell time at stations as well as access to the upper deck and ventilation generally. The two sets had a life of just over 20 years, invariably operating in multiple, and while clearly built to the maximum extremities of the loading gauge, there is still the familiar 'SR' family resemblance.

Introduced initially for stopping services concurrent with the Bournemouth line electrification, the 4VEP sets were a success from the outset and the type was eventually multiplied and could be found all over the electrified parts of the Southern Region. Boasting fast acceleration and reasonable comfort levels, albeit with 3+2 seating in what was then deemed '2nd Class', they were to be seen either singly or in multiple. There was one particular working where two 'VEP' sets plus a 'TC' and a Class 33 at the rear worked down from Waterloo as far as Basingstoke in the early evening. Here the train would split, with the two 'VEP' sets continuing towards Southampton while the '33' would propel the 'TC' over the non-electrified section to Salisbury. If you wanted a fast run out of Waterloo, this was the one to be on, with 1,000hp on each 'VEP' plus a further 1,550hp with the '33'. No wonder it invariably ran to time!

The Southern Way

The regular volume for the Southern devotee
MOST RECENT BACK ISSUES

The Southern Way is available from all good book sellers, or in case of difficulty, direct from the publisher. (Post free UK) Each regular issue contains at least 96 pages including colour content.

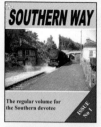
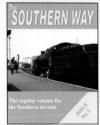

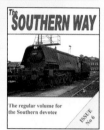
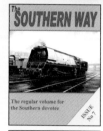
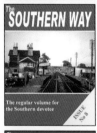

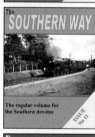
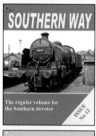
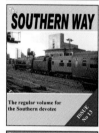
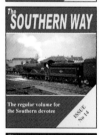
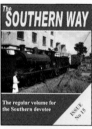
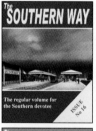
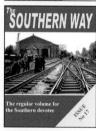

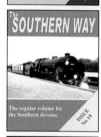
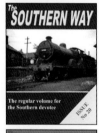

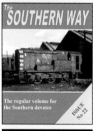
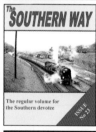
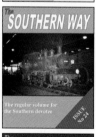
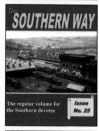
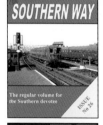

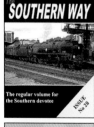
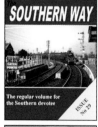

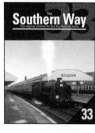
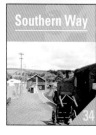
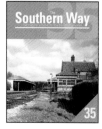

£11.95 each
£12.95 from Issue 7
£14.50 from Issue 21
£14.95 from Issue 35

Subscription for four-issues available
(Post free in the UK)
www.crecy.co.uk

96